D1384266

CITY ADRIFT

Also by Naresh Fernandes

Taj Mahal Foxtrot: The Story of Bombay's Jazz Age (2012)

CITY ADRIFT

A SHORT BIOGRAPHY OF
BOMBAY

÷

NARESH FERNANDES

ALEPH

ALEPH

ALEPH BOOK COMPANY
An independent publishing firm
promoted by *Rupa Publications India*

First published in India in 2013 by
Aleph Book Company
7/16 Ansari Road, Daryaganj
New Delhi 110 002

Copyright © Naresh Fernandes 2013

All rights reserved

No part of this publication may be reproduced,
transmitted, or stored in a retrieval system, in
any form or by any means, without permission
in writing from Aleph Book Company.

ISBN: 978-93-822-7720-0

1 3 5 7 9 10 8 6 4 2

This book is sold subject to the condition that
it shall not, by way of trade or otherwise, be
lent, resold, hired out, or otherwise circulated
without the publisher's prior consent in any form
of binding or cover other than that in which
it is published.

PART ONE

ONE

For months, the front pages had warned of imminent doom. Bombay was reeling under an explosion of 'pollution, crowds and noise', noted one pessimist. Predicted another, 'The urban landscape of Mumbai with its ever-increasing vehicular and population growth is a nightmare for everybody. And the nightmare will only worsen every year'.

Such a barrage of despair would have spooked the residents of most cities, but these forecasts were especially unnerving because they were contained in full-page advertisements aimed at getting people to pay outrageous amounts of money to actually live in Bombay. Every day, in *The Times of India* and *DNA*, in *Mid-Day* and the *Hindustan Times*, the real estate firms constructing Bombay's present were proclaiming with disarming candour that they had no faith in its future. But even as they expressed exasperation with the problems that were besetting contemporary Bombay, the developers proposed a simple solution: complete retreat.

They were encouraging residents to sequester themselves in housing complexes with names like Vasant Oasis ('reside at newer heights of happiness'), Rodas Enclave ('where a refreshing lifestyle flourishes') and Marathon NexZone ('next-generation eco-friendly Xtra utility homes').

Some of the housing complexes offered as sanctuaries bore names suggesting that they'd seceded from Bombay altogether. Kohinoor City in Kurla was in 'a class of its own'. Sports City in Thane was 'a mini metropolis that offers its residents world-class sporting facilities'. Rising City in Ghatkopar was 'the answer to Mumbai's need for space in a green environment'.

Amidst these expensive propositions for alternative cities, the pitch made for one complex in Wadala caught my eye for the artful manner in which it had appropriated one of the city's most resonant foundational myths. The headline of one of its advertisements gloated: 'The eighth island of Mumbai discriminates'. I needed to know more.

÷

As every schoolchild is taught, a large portion of contemporary Bombay has been conjured up over the centuries by reclaiming the tidal creeks separating the seven apocryphal islands that the Greeks are believed to have known as Heptanesia. This conjoined land was settled by the most diverse collection of people the subcontinent had ever known, who proceeded to create a mishmash culture that perfectly reflected their heterogeneity and verve.

This aspect of Bombay life can best be understood by eavesdropping on the conversations surging through its streets. When Bombayites pick arguments with, make purchases from or proposition strangers with

whom they share no common tongue, they do so in
an argot that amalgamates the syntax and vocabulary
of half a dozen linguistic traditions. It wraps Hindi,
Urdu, Gujarati, Marathi and English into the embrace
of a dialect Salman Rushdie named Hug-me. Bombay's
aptitude for aggregation can also be tasted in the snacks
sold on its footpaths: Chinese bhel, Schezwan idlis
and cheese dosas are made with ingredients (blended
together with a large dollop of enterprise) that share
the skillet only in this city. Even though these ensembles
seem ungainly to some, Bombay has, over the last two
hundred years, held India in thrall. For, in addition
to inventing snacks and slang, the proud denizens of
the metropolis reclaimed from ocean and iniquity have
specialized in producing a commodity that is rather
more incandescent. The city of interlocked islands, it's
widely acknowledged, is the place that manufactures
India's dreams.

The idea of India was born in Bombay in 1885,
when the Indian National Congress held its first meeting
in Gowalia Tank. The notion that workers deserved a
fair deal followed in 1890, when the first Indian trade
union was formed in the mill district. For a century,
the Bombay film industry has been projecting visions
of egalitarianism and meritocracy and love marriages
into the heartland, suggesting that any adversity can
be overcome if you work hard enough (and dance
around a tree in the appropriate fashion). To be fair,
not all Bombay fabrications have been salutary: since

the 1990s, the city's financial institutions and advertising agencies have seduced India's middle class into believing that greed is good, that empathy for the less fortunate is unnecessary, that extreme individualism is a virtue.

But that stream of dreams was running dry, or so said the property developer in Wadala. Bombay's ability to keep generating India's fantasies would be imperilled unless the city's geography was completely reconfigured. Luckily, help was at hand. Keeping 'the meteoric growth of the city in mind', the firm claimed to have constructed not just an eighth island but one that 'dwarfs' the other seven.

The twenty-nine-acre Island City Centre would be an 'exclusive integrated enclave' of 'branded residences' and serviced apartments, of business centres and shopping malls, that even had the capacity to 'expand time at will'. Freed from the morass of a traffic-snarled city, residents could 'pack a weekend into every weekday'. They would get private roads, temperature-controlled lobbies and separate service lifts to 'ensure that the service staff remains largely invisible'. Could I too 'discover a better life', as the copywriter had urged?

When I called to book an appointment, I was peppered with questions: Where did I work? How much did I earn? Where did I live? What was my budget? I declared proudly that I was a freelance journalist from Bandra who intended to spend Rs 3 crore on a flat, an unimaginably large sum of money that, I was certain, would single me out as a supremely desirable client. I was mistaken. The starting rate for flats in the complex, the representative sniffed, was Rs 6 crore. She promised to have someone call me back. No one ever did. As the headline had promised, the eighth island of Bombay *did* discriminate.

A week later, I rang again, assuming a rather more affluent persona. This time, I described myself as an editor instead of a journalist, and I assured them that I had Rs 7 crore to splash around. This gained me access to a darkened room on the edge of the construction site in which a well-produced video presentation was being screened. For about ten minutes, I was catapulted into a technicolour gated community with golf putting greens, motorized curtains and access-control restricted entry. It was clear that the Island City Centre would be 'a place where everyone [could] truly be everything that they imagined and more'.

After the presentation, a well-groomed executive in a deep black suit showed me floor plans for apartments in one of the buildings, an eighty-four-storey tower that would be a companion to an eighty-three-storey skyscraper. He handed me a thick brochure that matched the colour of his suit, and memos about payment schedules. On giant TV screens all around us, digital visualizations of Island City Centre ran on a loop. It was easy to imagine getting used to a place 'where business is discussed over a game of billiards and fine wine', but the starting price for a three-bedroom flat would take several hundred lifetimes of freelance journalism to cobble together. I downed the muddy Nescafé I'd been served by a liveried waiter, grabbed the black paper bag with the heavy brochure I'd been given and headed for the door. Even before I'd reached the gate, the fabric handles of the bag gave way. I tucked the package under my arm and trudged to the train station along a narrow pavement occupied by shanties.

÷

Over the past few years, I've spent many weekends trying to snatch visions of Bombay's future by making sweaty expeditions into its past. Though Bombay has always been in a state of change, the detritus of two millennia is just a train ride away. The region abounds with hero stones and dargahs, battlements and temples that preserve tableaux from a vanished city. When my bus trundles by the concrete drinking fountain in Kotwal Park opposite Plaza Cinema in Dadar, for example, I'm reminded of the pond that once occupied that stretch of green. But in addition to bringing into focus a water body that has long disappeared, the park, like many other Bombay relics, makes discernible things we've gained.

Every Sunday evening, the lawns around the pyau are steadily occupied by clusters of serious men. As the heat of the afternoon recedes, they flop down in small circles on the sparse grass. By around 5 p.m., dozens of intense, animated discussions can be witnessed everywhere. Each group is composed of men with roots in the same village in the Maharashtrian hinterland. When their families moved to the city a century ago, they lived in crowded chawls within an easy stroll of the park. The lawns were a comfortable location on which to catch up on news about home, arrange marriages and review the operations of the self-help schemes towards which everyone pooled in a little money. Though many of these families have since moved away to distant neighbourhoods, the filled-over pond, right by Dadar railway station, still proves a convenient rendezvous for scattered communities to come together for a few hours each weekend.

Of late, my walks have acquired a sense of urgency. I'm afraid that if I don't see these sights soon, they'll be demolished and I'll only have my collection of pictorial books to know them by. The metropolis I've reported on for most of my adult life has entered its most tumultuous period of transformation. Changes in land-use regulations have allowed real estate firms to begin construction on grasslands, farm plots and garbage dumps. In addition to this development, there's also 're-development'—the phrase in vogue to describe the phenomenon of older buildings and industrial estates being replaced by malls and glass towers. As Bombay soars higher, the shared spaces that made the city human—its pavements and playgrounds and beaches—are shrinking.

Bombay walks used to offer the pleasure of journeying through space and time. Now, neighbourhoods that echo with centuries of Bombay stories are being supplanted by buildings so intent on reflecting the latest global narratives, they have little to say about the lives on the streets around them. The preposterous property rates have even squeezed out Bombay's ghosts. The plots occupied by haunted houses have proved too valuable for them to be abandoned to the spirits.

More alarming are the woefully inadequate housing arrangements for the majority of the city's residents and the callousness towards the less fortunate that this reflects. Since 1991, the proportion of people living in slums has almost doubled: 48.5 per cent of Bombay's population of 12.4 million now lives in shanties. The informalization of Bombay's housing situation is, in part, a consequence of the disintegration of the manufacturing economy. As casual work, contract jobs and self-employment have become the order of the day, few working-class Bombay residents can hope to raise the money to move into usuriously priced—and scarce— legal homes. With the ocean of the disadvantaged swelling around them, increasing numbers of affluent Bombay residents are shutting themselves away in gated complexes like Island City Centre—incongruities in a metropolis whose most iconic structure is the Gateway of India, an announcement in yellow basalt that all settlers, no matter how tired or huddled, are welcome.

When it all gets overwhelming and I need a steady point from which to contemplate the city's ever-mutating form, I take a stroll to the Seaside Cemetery in Bandra, where my maternal great-grandfather is buried. The cemetery was hurriedly created in the closing years of the nineteenth century, when a bubonic plague epidemic was sweeping through Bombay. The disease would claim nearly 56,000 lives in the four years from 1896 and force hundreds of thousands to flee the city. But my family had nowhere to go. In a city of migrants, they were aboriginals, members of a geographically confused group of Roman Catholics who, even as they lived on the edges of the greatest city on India's west coast, called themselves East Indians.

The community had been converted to Catholicism in the sixteenth century and its members were initially known as Portuguese Christians, after the European power under which they had found their new faith. But in 1887, when Queen Victoria was celebrating the Golden Jubilee of her coronation, they decided to adopt a different identity. It was an era in which other groups of Roman Catholics, from Goa and Mangalore, were beginning to flock to Bombay. To distinguish themselves from these migrants, my mother's ancestors issued a proclamation informing the British sovereign of their desire to name themselves after the colonial trading firm, the East India Company. This, it would seem, was a rather gauche plea for clerical jobs in the colonial administration that they were sure would be the path to prosperity.

That anticipated affluence, or even a smidgin of comfort, was still a generation away when my great-

11

grandfather, Francis Xavier Rodrigues, succumbed to the plague bacillus, leaving behind a struggling wife, two daughters and a son. In family legend, Francis Xavier, who owned a tiny farm in the swampy neighbourhood of Khar, died a hero's death. At a time when fear of infection was rife, no one was willing to carry the bodies of the plague victims to the cemetery that had been established on the edge of the Arabian Sea, far enough from Bandra's hamlets to ensure that their inhabitants would not be exposed to additional contamination. My great-grandfather is said to have stepped up to the task of burying the dead, and paid for it with his life.

Since the 1990s, the Seaside Cemetery has seen its name rendered irrelevant. The tombstones have been marooned from the sea by staging yards for the ill-conceived Bandra-Worli Sea Link. But the soil retains its character: the high saline content ensures that corpses laid to rest here take an inordinately long time to decompose. Relatives who die in quick succession must be buried in temporary plots because digging open the family grave too soon is to risk finding the remains of the last occupant still intact. In this ever-changing city, memory persists in the oddest ways.

TWO

One humid October afternoon, I picked my way as unobtrusively as possible across the backyard of Colaba police station. The station house is situated opposite Leopold Cafe, where one evening four years earlier, two terrorists had opened fire on patrons enjoying their beer and finger chips, killing ten people and leaving several wounded. They were the vanguard of a group of ten men who would proceed to rampage through the Chhatrapati Shivaji railway station, a hospital, two hotels and a Jewish community centre in a three-day operation that would claim 161 lives. After all the violence, I'd anticipated tight security at the police station, but as it turned out, none of the uniformed men gave me a second look.

After sneaking around for about five minutes, I finally found what I was looking for: a pink plaque commemorating a battle with the sea. 'This tablet marks the site of the former crossing of about 300 yards of creek that separated the island of Bombay from Old Woman's Island', it declared. 'The creek was filled in 1838.'

Until then, the tongue of land that connected the lighthouse, lunatic asylum and military barracks on Old Woman's Island to the rest of the town was submerged at high tide. This resulted in a few inconveniences, reported Marianna Postans, a British traveller who visited Bombay the year the causeway was completed. 'Many have been the luckless wights, who, returning from a festive meeting, heedless of Neptune's certain visit, have found the curling waves beating over their homeward path, compelling them to seek again the "banquet hall deserted," or beg a shakedown at the quarters of their host,' she wrote. 'The more impetuous have sought to swim their horses across this dangerous pass... This inconvenience, so severely felt, led at length to the erection of a solid and handsome *valade*, with a foot-path protecting the elevated and level road.'

To many Bombay residents, the absence of solid connections between various components of the city was more than a mere inconvenience—journeying from one part of the city to another by boat could be positively lethal, especially during the monsoon. In 1837, the year before Mrs Postans visited, a monsoon gale had ripped ships from their moorings in the harbour and caused several deaths. Wrote one observer, 'Bombay really drowned that day'.

For much of its existence, the settlement had been defined by the patterns of the tide. 'Bombay is made up of five islands', one early description noted. 'As salt water creeks flow between them, the area is filled with mud. During low tide, one can see these five islands distinctly. However, during high tide, water rushes in and the islands then number seven.' The configuration of the estuary, geographers say, was constantly in flux.

Some sections became more prominent as tidal currents deposited silt on them, while others disappeared with erosion. The laborious process of knitting together the islands over the centuries not only made travel across the settlement less cumbersome, it altered Bombay's fate, transforming a malarial swamp into a global city. Today, roughly 40 per cent of the southern district known as 'the island city' and 20 per cent of the congested northern section of the metropolis, still known somewhat quixotically as 'the suburbs', consist of reclamations. For more than three centuries, land (or rather, the lack of it) and soil (especially the demands of those claiming to spring from it) have remained the city's preoccupations.

Strangely, Bombay has few official monuments to its slushy foundations. But in the cartography of everyday life, the ocean is rarely far away. It sloshes around in the names of landlocked neighbourhoods like the fig tree creek of Umerkhadi, washes against the vanished pier of Bori Bunder and surges at high tide through the drainage nallahs of Null Bazaar.

The islanded nature of old Bombay isn't difficult to detect if you know where to look. It manifests itself, for instance, in the disproportionate number of sixteenth-century Roman Catholic churches across the city, a profusion not strictly justified by the size of the Christian population of that era. However, the surfeit makes sense when you realize that when they were built, St Andrew's in Bandra, St Michael's in Mahim,

15

Our Lady of Salvation in Dadar, Gloria Church in
Byculla and Holy Name Cathedral in Colaba (the last
two relocated from older sites in the vicinity) stood
on separate islands and allowed their parishioners to
attend services without getting their feet wet.

÷

As naval officer K. R. U. Todd was taking a walk along
the shore of the rapidly expanding city of Bombay one
day in the early 1930s, he came upon a sight that must
have set his heart racing. A keen amateur archaeologist,
Todd chanced upon a shale hand axe that was perhaps
2.5 million years old. On subsequent visits to the site in
southwest Colaba, not so far from the police station, he
gathered fifty-five stone tools from the Early Palaeolithic
Age and a hundred and fifty scrapers, choppers and
blades from a slightly later period. In 1932, he reported
his findings in a paper titled 'Prehistoric Man Round
Bombay'.

Over the next few years, as a slew of modern
factories opened in the city, Todd devoted himself to
studying the millennia-old 'Palaeolithic Industries of
Bombay'. In an article with that title in *The Journal
of the Royal Anthropological Institute* in 1939, the
navy man proudly listed his additional findings: a beak-
shaped hand axe, the fossilized remains of a horse's
tooth, even shards of fired bowls with rounded rims. The
'coastal microliths as a whole appear... from their form,
patination and state of preservation to be definitely of

earlier date' than specimens he'd found on previous digs in central India, Todd wrote.

To augment his case that ancient man had lived in Bombay, however, Todd had to conduct his excavations more than thirty-five kilometres north of the spot at which he had found his first stone tools. As it turned out, the section of south Bombay in which Todd had made his initial discoveries had been in existence for less than a decade. It had been wrested from the Arabian Sea as a part of the Back Bay Reclamation Scheme of the 1920s, and the top filling for this swathe of 439 acres of new land between Churchgate and Colaba had been quarried from Padan Hill in distant Kandivali.

Todd learnt this after a fellow member of the Anthropological Society of Bombay, a senior civil service official named E. W. Perry, gave him official publications about the Back Bay scheme. Perry later took the lieutenant commander up to Kandivali himself. A photograph from one of Todd's expeditions shows him dressed in knee-length shorts, long socks and a sola topi, pointing to a particularly rich lode on the slopes of Padan Hill. In the reddish-brown gravel here, one to six feet under the surface, he recovered many treasures. 'Some of the specimens', Todd noted with satisfaction, 'are in mint condition'. From Todd's later recoveries, it's clear that Bombay's Stone Age ancestors got around quite a lot: the navy officer went on to collect microlithic implements in Versova, Manori and Pali Hill, establishing a much longer record of human habitation in the region than previously known. Through his digs, Todd had also proved that manufacturing and commerce were hardwired into the city's DNA.

By the second century BC, the action had come to be focused on the northern neighbourhood now known as Nalasopara, which had blossomed into a busy port that traded with Mesopotamia and Egypt. It was prominent enough to attract the attention of Emperor Ashoka, the Mauryan monarch who had converted to Buddhism. Edicts found here indicate that in the fourteenth year of his reign, the emperor dispatched preachers to the area. The remnants of a stupa still stand in Nalasopara and are, in typical Bombay fashion, the subject of a land dispute: an Adivasi woman has tenaciously resisted the effort of the Archaeological Survey of India to move her home away from the ancient mound of bricks, contending that her family has lived there for a century. When the case was heard in court, one judge asked the ASI to treat the woman with sympathy. 'Even Gautam Buddha renounced the world after seeing poverty and misery', he said.

The Buddha's message found eager acceptance in Bombay. Approximately 150 Buddhist and Brahmanical cave sites dating from the first century BC onwards have been identified in the region. These complexes served both as monasteries and rest houses for travelling merchants, evidence that the area's significance as a trading centre predated its British colonizers. So far, I've visited just over a dozen of these craggy sites, marvelling at how intelligently the men who built them used the contours of the terrain to create water harvesting systems and drainage channels. Not so long ago, I made my way to the highest point of the Kanheri Caves in Borivali, a set of 109 caverns that served as classrooms, dormitories and chapels for one of western India's most reputed ancient universities. It is located in the heart of the Sanjay Gandhi National Park, a nature reserve that has gained notoriety for its high population of leopards that occasionally kill humans. In recent years, housing complexes springing up on the perimeter of the 104-square-kilometre jungle have rendered the edges of the park increasingly impermeable, cutting the animals off from traditional migratory routes to other nearby reserves. At the same time, thousands of desperate families have built shanties inside the National Park. Their children have proved to be at high risk from attack, especially when they're squatting outdoors to defecate after dark; leopards have occasionally mistaken them for the small animals that are their regular prey.

From my vantage point atop the Kanheri Hills, I could see a vast swathe of the northern part of Bombay through which several cave sites stretched like the nodes of a web, out all the way down to the creek by Nalasopara, each complex perhaps half a day's walk from the other. Many are located along roads that are still in use centuries later, macadamized traces of ancient journeys. Some of the cave clusters consist of bare cells, completely lacking in ornament. Others, like Kanheri, dance with such intricate detail it's easy to understand why the sixteenth-century Portuguese historian Diogo do Couto concluded that it was 'one of the wonders—perhaps the greatest in the world'.

Over time, many of the complexes have been put to new use. The Mandapeshwar Caves in Borivali, for instance, bear both Shaivite motifs as well as a rough cross hewn by the Portuguese who built a church on the hill right above. For several years, a unit of policemen has been stationed in the musty cavern with a large pedestal fan for company, to prevent hotheads from renewing the debate centuries after that act of Catholic vandalism.

Other cave sites have been enfolded into slums, many of which have been built by neo-Buddhists—Dalits who followed the example of lower-caste leader B. R. Ambedkar when he embraced the faith in 1956. Depending on which way you want to see it, the caves are either a vibrant example of living history or a blatant act of encroachment. At Jogeshwari and Mahakali, hundreds of families have taken up residence around the monks' cells and on top of them. At the Magathane complex in Borivali, people actually live inside the caves. After a heritage-minded citizen filed a petition demanding protection for the site, the Archaeological Survey of India informed the High Court that it was too late to conserve it. The Court agreed with that opinion. The judges asked with an air of resignation, 'What is to be done now?'

I shared their despondency when I tramped through the Eksar neighbourhood in Borivali, looking for a clutch of thirteenth-century stones that depicted a pitched sea battle between Bombay's Silahara rulers and Yadava invaders. I'd learned about the memorials in a scholarly journal, which suggested that the figurines on the rock represented warriors squabbling for control of the port of Sopara. (The Silahara leader Someswara drowned defending his kingdom and Bombay was lost.) The article, published in 1984, said that the six stones stood on the banks of a pond amidst a mango orchard. When I finally found the place, there were neither fruit trees nor pond to be seen. Instead, the concrete foundations of a residential tower were sprouting from a deep pit.

The memorial stones, we learned, had been placed in an open-air shrine built within the confines of the complex and it took a little pleading before the security guards allowed us in. The relics were as magnificent as the journal had promised. Two of them stood about eight feet high, their faces brimming with ships and warriors, gods and horsemen. Studying the intricacies of the long-forgotten oceanic battle, it was impossible to ignore the scrimmages of the present. Here, on the edges of the city, a developer had appropriated a sliver of Bombay's memory and triumphantly christened the complex Aquaria Grande.

I wasn't quite so fortunate in my quest for the next stage of the Bombay story. I spent two weekends looking for Raja Bhim, who is thought to have arrived in the islands in the thirteenth century after being dislodged from his kingdom, probably in Gujarat. Under him, the islands experienced their first growth spurt. According to the ancient chronicle *Bimbakyan*, or History of Bhim, the king built palaces for himself and his officials, encouraged the cultivation of coconut palms and introduced several fruit-bearing species to the islands. Just as significantly, he added to the diversity of the settlement by bringing along an entourage that included Kunbis and Bhandaris, Yajurvedi Brahmans and Pathare Prabhus.

Apparently, the descendants of his followers have kept his memory alive by setting up a temple with 'a black stone, besmeared with red ochre and adorned with flowers, to which they offer, at certain seasons, milk, butter, fruits, and even goats and fowls'—or so one colonial text said tantalizingly. The book was rather specific about the location of the shrine: it was in the neighbourhood of Naigaum, in a pocket known as 'Bhima Raja's Wady', very near where Island City Centre was emerging. I spent hours looking for it. There was no dearth of advice. Helpful locals guided me to temples across Naigaum, Wadala and nearby Parel, but these shrines turned out to be dedicated to Shiv, Jari Mari, Dattatreya, Hanuman, Wagheswari and Chandika Devi. On a side street leading up Golanji Hill, I chanced upon a stunning three-metre-tall monolith with seven representations of Shiva, perhaps one for each of the city's original islands. It dated back to the sixth century. The priest in the temple next door (a legal advisor at an advertising firm by day) told me that his family had served at the shrine for eleven generations, but he'd never heard of Bhim Raja. It was most baffling. The colonial text had said that 'the spirit of the old monarch still haunts, still watches over the lands for which he did so much and upon which he set an ineradicable seal'. But the temple dedicated to Bhim Raja had vanished.

Much more resolute than the shrine, however, are the Kolis, the fishing people who are thought to have been the sole inhabitants of the islands until Bhim Raja's arrival. Eight centuries later, the Kolis continue to ply their trade on the city's shores, though with increasing difficulty. The metropolis discharges 365 million metric tonnes of raw sewage into the sea each year, to the detriment of its marine life. Even the Bombay duck, the succulent lizardfish so closely associated with these waters, has become scarce. Fishermen now have to travel eight hours or more off the coast to fill their nets.

The Kolis have come to be seen as anachronisms in a city that dreams of being 'world-class', unmindful of the fact that other modern metropolises such as New York and Hong Kong are still home to people who make their living casting their nets into the sea. The last century has seen Kolis expelled from beaches such as Chowpatty on which they landed their boats, while reclamations have divorced fishermen from the water in Bandra, Dharavi and Sion. Some Koli settlements have come to be perceived as slums, even as their prime seaside locations have made them the target of developers. Despite the odds, they cling to their livelihoods doggedly, aided, perhaps, by their primal deities.

I stumbled upon one mighty Koli goddess in the backyard of the Colaba police station, right next to the plaque marking the creation of the Causeway. She manifested herself in a jagged hunk of black rock, adorned with green vestments and vermillion. A book on Bombay's temples published in 1900 noted that the shrine stood near the tram stables. 'Different sorts of vows are made to the [idol]', the book said. 'Fowls and he-goats are offered to [it].' Animal sacrifices are rare these days, but fresh flowers on the ground confirmed that the idol is still revered.

Like the inscription on the plaque next to it, the compact temple speaks lucidly of the city's transformations. Though the Arabian Sea crashes into a promenade more than two hundred metres away now, the rock continues to be worshipped with coconuts and marigolds as Khadi Devi—the Goddess of the Creek.

THREE

The modern city of Bombay owes its genesis to a dream of three goddesses. They appeared to a government contractor named Ramji Shivaji one night in the early 1770s, as the authorities struggled to build an embankment connecting Bombay with Worli. At that time, the sea swept through the great breach between these islands 'with all the fury and pleasure of an Arabian colt', as one observer put it, across the Byculla flats to Bhendi Bazaar and beyond. Travellers from Mahim and Parel would break their journeys to dip their toes in the spume at Pydhonie, the foot wash, even as the waves galloped on to Umerkhadi.

At that time, though several inlets between the island cluster had been filled up, Bombay was still a rather primitive place, so backward that windowpanes in some homes were made from translucent seashell instead of from glass, sniffed Govind Narayan, the city's earliest biographer, in a book published in 1863. He was not alone in believing that the stagnation was a consequence of Bombay's archipelagic geography. The vapours emanating from the swamps, it was commonly suggested, caused rampant disease and inhibited prosperity.

When William Hornby took over as governor in 1771, he was convinced that closing the breach between the islands with a vellard—a word derived from the Portuguese vellado for 'hedge' or 'fence'—would improve the city's sanitary conditions as well as its economic outlook by adding 40,000 acres of cultivable land to it. But the directors of the East India Company refused to sanction the enterprise, claiming that the Rs 1 lakh he had requested for it was extravagant. Hornby decided to defy them and proceeded with the vellard towards the end of his term. In the days of sail mail, he knew he'd be able to fill the breach before the directors could interfere.

However, it wasn't as straightforward as Hornby hoped it would be. Though boats kept dumping stones into the ocean for a seawall, the dike refused to hold. That's when the goddesses Mahalaxmi, Mahakali and Mahasaraswati told the engineer Ramji Shivaji their secret. They said that when Sultan Mubarak Shah's men captured Bombay in 1318, they had fled their ancient haunts in Worli to hide in the creek, the Kshirsagar. If the 'milk was separated from the sea' and they were brought back to dry land, they promised that the seawall would hold. Ramji cast his net in the waters and rescued the deities. Mahalaxmi, the Goddess of Wealth, was soon installed in a grand temple that still stands on the shore, and she showered the emerging city with her blessings.

'The building of the embankment changed the fortunes of Bombay', Govind Narayan wrote. 'In one stroke, the creek which swamped half of Mumbai was dammed and Bombay was converted into a veritable Lanka.' He marvelled, 'Is it not an astounding feat to recover land from the sea and make it habitable and free of disease and earn lakhs of rupees in the process?'

Bombay's prospects, it's clear, had brightened a little since 1661, when the Crown had acquired Bombay as part of Charles II's marriage settlement with the Portuguese princess Catherine of Braganza. The princess, it appeared, was not exactly the most pulchritudinous candidate on hand. The first time Charles met Catherine, he is said to have exclaimed, 'My God! They have brought me a bat' to marry. Perhaps anticipating some hesitation on this score, the Portuguese had tried to sweeten the deal by offering Charles the largest dowry the world had ever known. The enticements of the Treaty of Whitehall included Tangier in North Africa, trading privileges in Brazil and the East Indies, and two million cruzados. The Portuguese also threw in the islands of Bombay, which they had acquired in 1534 from the sultan of Gujarat. This clinched the deal, though it couldn't ensure marital affection. Charles would go on to sire at least twelve children—none of them with Catherine.

I learned about Catherine's woes in great detail in the mid-1990s when I was living in New York, whose most iconic district, Manhattan, is, like Bombay, a peninsula that makes a disproportionate contribution to creating the myths of the nation in which it is situated. New York's Portuguese community had suddenly realized that Catherine was the monarch commemorated in the name of the borough of Queens (and that her husband was referenced in the official name of Brooklyn: King's County). To celebrate that connection, New York's Portuguese decided to erect a 50-foot bronze statue of Catherine on the far bank of the river that flows past the United Nations building, her hair and dress billowing in the gentle breeze. An organization called Friends of Queen Catherine raised $1.6 million for the undertaking and commissioned a sculptor to create a maquette.

But months before the figure could be cast, some African-American groups began to protest. They claimed that Catherine was a slave owner—or that, at any rate, she had married into a family that had benefitted from the trade in humans. 'Catherine has a sordid past,' Betty Dopson, the leader of a group called Friends Against Queen Catherine, told me. 'Her hands are bloody with the murder of millions of Africans.' Irish activists soon joined the fray, saying that Catherine's family had been the cause of the Potato Famine that killed tens of thousands of people in Ireland. 'The statue is a symbol of imperialism, of the subjugation of native people,' thundered an activist named Eedie Cuminale. 'It's a blot to build a statue of a monarch in a country that prides itself on its democratic traditions.'

The plans to erect the statute were abandoned, much to the dismay of Manuel Andrade e Sousa, the man who had dreamt up the idea. 'Queen Catherine was

an immigrant who travelled to a strange land and had
to face the problems that all immigrants in New York
face,' he said. 'She was a victim of seventeenth-century
prejudice and we can't judge her by the standards of
the twentieth century.'

In death, as in life, Catherine didn't have an easy
time. Her husband's disdain for his marital duties was
matched by his aversion to the prospect of governing
Bombay, which, he had been given to understand, was
'within a very little distance of Brazil'. In 1668, he
leased Bombay to the East India Company for a rent
of ten pounds per annum, to be paid 'in gold, on the
30th day of September, yearly, forever'.

Upon taking control of the islands, the Company
made a great show of convincing Charles II that
they'd done him a favour by relieving him of a 'great
burthen and expense'. One official claimed that the
firm had been saddled with a 'beggarly, ruined' land.
Even Samuel Pepys, chief secretary to the admiralty, in
his famous *Diary*, described Bombay as a 'poor little
island' and scoffed at the 'inconsiderableness of the
place'. The carping continued for years afterwards.
When a British East India Company chaplain named
John Ovington dropped by a little later, he complained
that the insalubrious climate made the settlement seem
like 'no more than a parish graveyard, a charnel house',
in which for Europeans, 'two monsoons are the age
of a man'.

In truth, the East India Company had long coveted

Bombay, especially in the face of the restrictions they faced at their trading post in Surat in Gujarat, which they had held at the indulgence of the Mughals since 1613. In the well-sheltered port of Bombay, the British could construct fortifications to secure their mercantile privileges without offending the emperor of Hindustan, effectively dominating India's western coast. Having leased a portion of the Queen's dowry, they were at liberty, Governor Gerald Aungier declared in 1672, to lay out 'a city which by God's assistance is intended to be built'.

It isn't clear which deities were consulted in the expansion of the fishing town of Bombay, but the city that emerged over the next 150 years was well designed to facilitate the profit-making objectives of a joint stock multinational corporation such as the East India Company. The city's layout, as well as the regulations about land use and land sales, was conceptualized not to enhance the comfort of residents but to maximize commercial gain. Aungier had been reminded by the firm's directors in London: 'Our business is to advantage ourselves by trade and what government we have is but the better to carry on and support that.'

Like a good real estate developer, Aungier set out to augment the value and appeal of his property. The nucleus of the settlement was an old house that had once belonged to Garcia da Orta, a Portuguese Jewish physician who had been granted possession of the islands around 1554. Da Orta had a pretty garden with a section of medicinal plants he used for his research. His extensive library contained the works of Hippocrates, Aristotle, Galen and St Augustine. Around this shrine to knowledge in the present-day Naval Dockyard, the East India Company built battlements, both seaward and landward, and gates to control movement. A militia of Bhandaris, a community that until then had made their living brewing liquor, was raised to ensure security. Just as significantly, a Supreme Court of Judicature was constituted to guarantee rule of law, especially with regard to disputes over contracts and the other matters that were essential for business to thrive.

Even as an embryonic settlement of 10,000 people, Bombay displayed a talent for vacillation that would persist all the way into the twenty-first century. After a conflagration destroyed three hundred homes in 1671, the Company decided to use the opportunity to rebuild the town using cutting-edge urban design principles evolved in London after the Great Fire of 1666. A copy of the Rebuilding of London Act, which had laid down minimum construction standards, was dispatched to Bombay. The Company decided that the fire-ravaged homes belonging to Koli fisherfolk and traders should be rebuilt in stone with tiled roofs, on regularly aligned streets. But soon, Bombay's administrators concluded that building in stone was too expensive and postponed the housing initiative. Instead, the stone and lime mortar was diverted to constructing the Fort, warehouses, a granary and public buildings.

Since trade was the company's main concern, customs duties were waived on both imports and exports to stimulate business. In those early years, coconuts and coir were the dominant commodities. Though the Company also started dealing in textiles, the product that would later become the mainstay of Bombay's economy, its initial experience with the cloth business was not encouraging. The residents of the tropics proved impervious to the attractions of English broadcloth and woollens.

Despite these disappointments, the Company realized that it had another vehicle to fatten its bottom line: land revenues. The governor set about trying to reconcile the numerous patterns of land leases that abounded on the islands, some established by the Portuguese, others more ancient. The Portuguese had collected one-fourth of each estate owner's crops as a cess. After meeting with the territory's largest landholders, Aungier decided to establish a less cumbersome land tax instead.

Early in its occupation of the islands, the Company realized that it could expand its real estate holdings by 'recovering the overflown lands'. The Company's Surat Council informed their superiors in London that the sea overran a third of their new territory during high tide, 'making soe much wast ground that is noe way usefull but a great annoyance'. However, 'the coming in is narrow', they noted, 'and in the judgement of sober men is easie to be kept out'. They predicted that if bunds were built, in three years, 'it will make good arable land as any uppon the island'.

These proposals weren't at all far-fetched. The draining of the marshy Fens in eastern England in the 1630s proved that the task wasn't impossible. Besides, seized by the Renaissance conviction that Man had a duty to wrestle Nature into submission, Bombay's administrators believed that the tidal creeks were theirs for the taking: after all, these were 'drowned', 'overflown' and 'flooded' lands, all waiting redemption. However, when Aungier undertook an inspection tour of the flooded lands at Worli, Mahim and Dharavi in 1670, he realized that the proposition would be more expensive than imagined. In a notable Bombay precedent, he postponed the work and appointed a committee to estimate exactly how much it would cost. In the meantime, a surveyor measured the drowned lands and mapped out four crucial breaches that would need to be filled in for reclamation to be effective. In 1675, the Company suggested a build-operate-transfer model, offering private parties that drained the flooded lands ninety-nine-year leases to the property. Nine years later, it mulled over a plan to pay workers in both rice and cash.

Over the next decades, dikes were built to drain the inlets between the northernmost islands. The dam between Sion and Dharavi was made of stone filled with 'firm fast clay and rubbish', said John Burnell, an English sailor who visited it in 1710. The top was 'covered with a gravelly sand, which makes a most pleasant walk'. The seawall between Dharavi and Mahim was not so imposing: 'It is something more than half the length of the other,' he reported. Reclamation work had also started between Mahim and Worli. 'When I left the island, they were damming up this break,' Burnell wrote, 'designing to go through with all that remains open to the ocean's invasion.'

Even as he began to create new land, Aungier set about assembling a new citizenry for the town in the making, paying special heed to wooing members of trading castes to the commercial centre he was hoping to build. Banias from the Deccan and diamond merchants from Surat were offered a range of enticements to settle in Bombay. An official petition relating to Nima Parakh, a bania from Diu, shows how generous the incentives were. To encourage him to relocate, Parakh was offered money to build a home, free movement to and from the Fort, immunity from being arrested without notice and an exemption for his family from watch-and-ward duty.

Though the Company's attempts to sell imported textiles had failed, it didn't stop them from seeking to profit from the high demand for Indian calicoes and cottons in Europe. Weavers from the nearby towns of Thana and Bhiwandi were invited to Bombay. In 1669, new houses were built on a street between the Fort and the customs house for weavers from Chaul, the former Portuguese settlement a little to the south. Concessions were even offered to foreign merchants:

Armenian traders were afforded warehousing facilities and exempted from anchorage charges.

However, another experiment in attracting migrants went a little awry. Administrators began to import Englishwomen to marry British settlers, but some of the women had quickly 'grown scandalous', prompting the authorities to 'give them fair warning that they do apply themselves to more sober and Christian conversation'. If the women failed to heed this advice, they were to be confined to their vessels and fed only bread and water until they were shipped back to England.

Just seven years after the Company took over the islands, Bombay's population was estimated to have jumped to 60,000. When a British doctor named John Fryer visited Bombay in 1673, he was struck by the diversity of the town, 'in which confusedly lived' English, Portuguese, Topazes of mixed Indian and Portuguese extraction, Muslims, Hindus, Koli Christian fishermen and Bhandaris who tended the coconut palms. Other records from the time are more detailed, noting the presence of several groups of Muslims who worked as artisans, traders and seamen; Hindu traders, Prabhu farmers and rent collectors, rice-cultivating Kunbis, Shenvi farmers and traders; and Parsis, 'an industrious people and ingenious in trade, wherein they totally employ themselves'.

Already, the incipient city carried the promise of equal opportunity that would make it different from any other settlement India had known. Tolerance was the hallmark of Bombay, a virtue that Charles II had enjoined the Company to uphold. 'You are to suffer [Indians] to enjoy the exercise of their own religion without the least intervention or discountenance', he commanded. Gerald Aungier had much to do with creating the ethic that would define Bombay for more than three hundred years. On 8 August 1672, the day on which Portuguese law was officially superseded by British law, the governor urged his judge to ensure that justice would be available to all, 'without fear [or] favour' on the island that was inhabited by 'severall nations and religions'. In particular, he enjoined the judge to guarantee fair treatment for 'even the meanest person of the Island, and particular the Poore, the Orphan, the Widow and the Stranger in all matters of controversy'. Though it never quite achieved this ambition, it was one that Bombay would cherish for much of its existence—until it suddenly turned its back on its history in the 1990s.

÷

In official chronicles and travellers' accounts of the rise of Bombay, Indian voices are conspicuously absent. But of course, it would be too much to expect Indians to allow themselves to be written out of the story. They were simply too argumentative to be silenced completely. Every now and then, the disputations of Bombay's oldest inhabitants appear between the cracks—in petitions, representations and acts of stubbornness, reminding their rulers of the flaws in their perfect plans. Not surprisingly, many of the conflicts related to land. (Centuries later, many continue to defy resolution.)

Among the earliest confrontations on record was a fracas, curiously enough, over manure. Bombay's Kunbi community had traditionally used rotten fish—known as kut—to enhance the yields of their fields. This practice dismayed the British, who were convinced that the fishy odour caused life-threatening diseases. 'The buckshawing or dunging of toddy trees with fish occasions in great measure the unwholesome of the Bombay air', a letter from the Court to the government claimed in 1708. The British visitor Dr Fryer begged to differ, attributing the poor health of the British to their frequent dalliances with 'foul women' and excessive consumption of 'fool rack', a kind of brandy he believed was made with fish blubber. (In reality, it was phool arak, or liquor distilled from palm sap.) Dr Fryer's diagnosis was ignored. In 1704, the authorities decided to prohibit the practice of buckshawing on a large part of Bombay island.

But the deliberations continued for decades. In 1736, a group of landholders told the government that the fish manure ban had forced several Kunbis to abandon Bombay and move to Salsette island. 'The trees cannot produce fruit, or thrive, grow or benefit by any other sort of manure', the citizens claimed. 'Their produce decreases daily so as to have arrived at the last extremity of ruin, to the great loss of your petitioners.'

The landlords offered to pay the government Rs 1,000 annually if it lifted the restrictions. The President of the Board acknowledged that agricultural productivity had indeed declined since the imposition of the ban, but noted that the settlement was healthier than ever. He declined to withdraw the order, choosing 'the health of the inhabitants of the islands to the profit...proprietors of lands might make by the use of kut'. For years after this, the landlords continued to petition, the government flip-flopped and the practice of using dry fish as manure for coconut trees persisted well into the 1990s, until farmland in the northernmost neighbourhoods was finally absorbed by the encroaching city.

Other disputes were decidedly more urban (and enduring), such as the demand for fairer compensation from people whose plots of land had been acquired by the authorities for infrastructural work. Bombay's first megaproject was the construction of a town wall and other fortifications. The Company's directors in London were loath to sanction any money for public improvements, since every rupee spent was a rupee less in dividends for them. But fear of attack from the French and the Marathas led to fortifications being constructed and strengthened in stages. In 1739, funds to dig a protective ditch were raised by merchants setting aside 1 per cent of the value of their trade. But people who had to surrender their land and trees for the moat were not satisfied with their remuneration.

The disgruntled citizens included Vithaldas Kasidas,

who complained that he'd been underpaid for the 201 coconut trees he'd lost. He had been given Rs 4 per tree, but the rate, he contended, should actually have been double, since the value of trees had been rising since the bank established by the Company had begun to lend money to anyone who could put up land as security. Kasidas was eventually allotted another holding. A few years later, there was long-drawn-out correspondence about the valuation of a plot on the Back Bay acquired from the widow of Fakir Shaw Janulla. In the end, her plot was also accorded a higher value, though it isn't clear from the records whether the parcel of land she received as compensation was to her satisfaction. Their arguments foreshadowed by 230 years the prolonged correspondence my maternal grandfather, Ammon Rodrigues, the son of Francis Xavier Rodrigues, would have with the authorities when they acquired his small farm in 1959, ostensibly for the construction of a public maternity hospital.

But the yelps of these individual skirmishes would soon get lost in the clamour of the larger battle that the city's authorities fought with purported encroachers. In 1754, administrators grumbled that several inhabitants of the town had 'erected sheds and buildings without license' on the main streets. To ensure that this would not be repeated, a set of building regulations was promulgated—and announced in public to the beating of a drum so that no one could plead ignorance of them. The code forbade walls or sheds from being constructed within the limits of the town before permission had been received (a directive contemporary real estate developers routinely disregard; they have long realized that these violations can, for a consideration, be 'regularized' by the authorities). Illegal hutments and upper floors were to be demolished. 'If anyone presumes to act in contempt of the above regulations', the administrators threatened, 'he shall be subject to such penalty as the Honourable President and Council pleases to inflict'.

Twenty-five years later, the authorities were still attempting to impose a sense of order on the town. While they'd managed to get residents to stay within their designated plots, they'd forgotten to rule on an important matter of city planning: the heights of buildings. As a result, many Indians had taken the opportunity 'to raise their houses to so great a height as may be injurious to the healthiness of the town', administrators noted. They weren't sure how to immediately remedy the problem. But, summing up the central axiom of urban life, they expressed optimism that 'a cure might be effected in a moderate time...by proper regulations rigidly adhered to—since in all well-regulated communities, the conveniency of an individual must give way to public good'. It's a lesson Bombay is still struggling to grasp.

FOUR

Shortly after Mahalaxmi was enthroned in her temple, the town whose surface and society had been fitted together like a jigsaw puzzle began to weave the legends that would set it apart from every other Indian city. It would soon declare itself to be *Urbs Prima in Indis*— India's First City.

By 1775, it all seemed to be coming along rather nicely. That year, a passing merchant named Abraham Parsons wrote very admiringly of the sections of Bombay that lay within the walls of the Fort, especially its spacious Green. 'The streets are well laid out and the buildings so numerous and handsome as to make it an elegant town', he wrote. Around the same time, a civil servant named James Forbes listed some of Bombay's most imposing structures: the Government House, customs house, mint, treasury, prison, an Anglican church, three hospitals, a charity school for boys and a theatre. That wasn't all. A new dock had been built at Mazagaon, the police system was reorganized and plans drawn up to improve the town's drainage. In 1780, the population had touched 113,726—a precise figure that had been established by a survey to calculate how much food would be needed in that year of scarcity.

But 1803 brought a tragedy. A savage fire swept through a section of the town, destroying three-fourths of the bazaar, the customs house and 471 homes. One section of opinion believed that the conflagration was a display of wrath by the Pandavas, incensed by the beauty of a wedding tent erected by a cotton merchant. Nothing so splendid had been seen on earth since the five brothers had ascended to the heavens, and they were not willing to be upstaged. (Others maintained that the fire had been sparked by a cooking accident.) The blaze was the excuse for administrators to relocate some Indian homes outside the walls of the town, especially if their owners had businesses that involved oil, bitumen, ghee and other flammable substances. Their homes formed the nucleus of the neighbourhoods that would constitute the Native Town and established a geographical conundrum that still vexes Bombay: though the metropolis races further north with each decade, the district acknowledged as the city centre continues to be located at its southern tip.

While Bombay now had many essential pieces in place, it was a series of events ten years after the fire that really allowed the town to flourish. In 1813, the British parliament withdrew the East India Company's monopoly on trade with the subcontinent, encouraging the formation of more agency houses and firms, many of them Indian. Five years later, the British annexation of the Peshwa's territories after the Third Anglo-Maratha War guaranteed smooth passage for the produce of the hinterland to the port of Bombay, a process that was accelerated when the Bhor Ghat road was constructed over the Western Ghats in 1830. Cotton exports began to grow, especially after 1832, when American cotton prices rose.

In 1838, when the Colaba Causeway was completed, Bombay stood on the springboard of history. As the diarist Mrs Postans was wandering wide-eyed through the Isle of Palms, a first generation of Indians was receiving a Western-style education in English; literary and scientific societies were being formed;, and newspapers, in English, Gujarati, Urdu and Marathi, were gaining readers. In addition, steam navigation had brought European ideas and goods within a six-week journey of the city. A swelling middle class of teachers, clerks and translators who called themselves Young Bombay would soon assume crucial roles in civic and intellectual institutions. 'Few places have undergone greater change and improvement...during the last six years' as Bombay has, Mrs Postans wrote, 'and if we venture to become prophetic...its career of progress promises to be even yet more singularly rapid'.

Much of that velocity was generated by the town's expanding links with China, a country that couldn't get enough of a commodity that Bombay now pretends it never sold: opium. Between 1830 and 1860, there was a tenfold increase in exports of the narcotic through the city's bustling port. Over the next few decades, China, as the title of one book put it, would be the making of Bombay—though, as another historian has contended, the city's foundations actually lie in the opium plantations of Bihar. Either way, the enormous profits of the China Trade would, in a few decades, provide the seed capital for opium traders to create shipping, banking and industrial empires. Many of the families that opened cotton textile mills in the city later in the century got their start in the opium trade. At the end of the twentieth century, they would cash in the land on which their looms stood and enter the real estate business. It is now fashionable to claim that the China Traders were unaware of the devastation the narcotic caused its users, but that's implausible: after all, the Chinese had fought two Opium Wars to try to stop the drug shipments.

The most famous China Trader was Jamsetjee Jejeebhoy, a poor Parsi who came to Bombay (after his father died young) to work with his uncle, a bottle seller. Jejeebhoy's ascent to untold wealth was instrumental in spawning that oft-repeated Bombay cliché—that migrants come to the city hoping to make enormous fortunes (even though most merely hope to find steady jobs). Of course, Jejeebhoy's contribution to Bombay was much greater than this inspirational rags-to-riches story. Acknowledging his position of immense privilege amidst widespread poverty, Jejeebhoy and his peers constructed a tradition that set Bombay apart from other Indian cities: jaw-droppingly munificent public philanthropy.

Long before business houses constituted special departments to oversee their 'corporate social responsibility' activities (and attendant tax breaks),

Jejeebhoy and other merchant princes used their profits from the China Trade to endow ambitious institutions of learning and healing, as well as quotidian amenities such as drinking water fountains. Bombay's opium traders were a cosmopolitan group: they included Parsis, Konkani Muslims, Gujaratis, Goan Catholics and Baghdadi Jews. Two centuries later, many of their names—Wadia, Sassoon, Jehangir, Petit—are still familiar to Bombay from the marble plaques on the institutions they funded.

The concern they demonstrated for creating public infrastructure and a public culture in Bombay has, unfortunately, evaporated in the era of globalized capital. Though Bombay is now home to nine of the fifteen richest Indians and has the world's seventh-highest concentration of high-net-worth individuals, these newly minted billionaires have made little effort to improve the quality of life in a city they share with twelve million others—even though they presumably breathe the same grimy air and crawl through the traffic on the same congested roads. To modern-day Bombay's great loss, transnational capital controlled by businessmen with residence rights in multiple locations has no local allegiance.

Of all of the merchant princes, Sir JJ's memory is most revered. Jejeebhoy's first recorded act of charity occurred in 1822, when he spent Rs 3,000 to repay the loans taken by several men jailed for debt. Over the decades, Jejeebhoy money would fund all sorts of

45

endeavours, including a causeway between Bandra and Mahim that, in 1845, would consolidate the island's links with the mainland. During his lifetime, Jejeebhoy would spend Rs 2.5 million on charity, his benevolence eventually earning him a baronetcy. The institutions most closely associated with him are the JJ School of Art and the JJ Hospital where a statue of the patron still presides over a hallway. Many poor patients look upon the life-sized black metal figure as a representation of the divine, and leave offerings of flowers and fruit at his feet. Not so long ago, plans to give the statue a makeover ran into a rumpus when the authorities ignored a suggestion of the hospital employees who have to deal with the consequences of the great reverence for the old China Trader. Their irate leader told journalists, 'We had asked for a drainage system at the foot of the statue for coconuts that are broken in Sir JJ's honour, but that wasn't done.'

The energetic movement between Bombay and China not only enlivened the landscape with impressive buildings, it also moulded cultural tastes. Ships returning from the east carried porcelain articles at the bottom of their holds because these items were waterproof and made good ballast. Blue Chinese plates and vases found their way into the homes of many Bombayites, both rich and middle class. Chinese silks, jade and paintings became commonplace. Peonies, plum blossoms and other Chinese motifs burst into bloom on the silk gara saris worn by Parsi women. The patterns of the

Middle Kingdom could also be seen in the tanchoi technique for weaving silk brocade, which is said to have been introduced to India by three brothers from Surat dispatched to China by Jamsetjee Jejeebhoy. The name is thought to reflect the fact that the three (or 'tan' in Gujarati) received instruction from a Chinese master weaver named Choi.

The city's new consuming class were soon purchasing fragile luxuries from even further away. In September 1834, the *Darpan* newspaper reported that a ship had arrived from Boston laden with 'frozen water', in slabs six inches thick, cut from a New England river. The cargo had been shipped in by Frederic Tudor, an American entrepreneur who had found a market niche selling ice to the overheated people of the tropics. An ice house costing Rs 10,000, raised by public subscription, was constructed next to the Scots Kirk opposite the docks. It had 'double walls of plank, the hollow space between them filled with cotton, through which substance heat penetrates with great difficulty', *Darpan* reported. Even though about 50 tonnes of the 180-tonne cargo had melted en route, 'a very large portion will remain for the use of the Bombay community', the paper cheered. Jamsetjee Jejeebhoy was the first person to serve ice at a dinner party, though the *Bombay Samachar* reported a few days later that the host and many of his guests caught colds.

The vast fortunes of the China Traders ensured that Bombay, unlike many other colonial cities, would be fashioned substantially by the visions of Indians. They were offered places on administrative and judicial bodies, serving as Justices of Peace and as members of the Board of Conservancy. When the municipal corporation was created a little later, the shetias had a significant presence on it. Their enormous assets allowed the merchants to stand as relative social equals to Europeans, as a consequence of which Bombay was less racially segregated than Calcutta or Madras. Traders such as the Banajis, the Amichunds and the Jejeebhoys were able to build mansions within the walls of the Fort—Bombay's original gated community. For poorer Indians, though, who lived at the northern end of the Fort and in the Native Town, cramped homes and cholera were a way of life.

On the afternoon of 16 April 1853, another element of the Bombay story fell into place when a steam locomotive snorted out of the railway station at Bori Bunder. Artillery guns boomed a salute and the governor's band struck up the British national anthem. As the train bedecked with bunting moved along its course to Thane, thirty-four kilometres away, 'the whole line was densely crowded with spectators', reported the *Bombay Times*, since a holiday had been declared to allow residents to witness history in the making. The gradually expanding railway network would provide the frame for Bombay's growth, a phenomenon that has continued all the way into the twenty-first century.

In the train compartments would emerge an easy

urbanity as people from different castes and communities were forced to share benches and, in current times, are wedged together in positions of daring intimacy. This is only to be expected when 5,000 commuters are stuffed into trains built to carry 1,800—a density that the authorities describe as the 'super-dense-crushload'. The commonplace negotiations of the commute—such as the convention of allowing a fourth traveller to sit on a bench built for three, but only on one buttock—force an acknowledgement of other people's needs.

Bombay seemed to be so focused on its own journey, it was almost untouched by the uprising that swept through much of north India in 1857, even though it was not entirely free of Wahhabi phobia—the panic about the massacres Muslim insurgents were rumoured to be plotting. The Anglo-Indian police chief Charles Forjett slipped into disguise to eavesdrop on bazaar conversations and scotched the plans of a group of alleged conspirators. One afternoon shortly afterwards, two of them were lashed to the mouths of cannons on the Esplanade. 'Our pulses throbbed faster and faster till at a given word of command the cannons were fired and the pinioned criminals were blown', one Indian observer recalled. 'The burnt flesh sent an unpleasant odour which we could all easily sniff. All was over.'

A few months later, on 1 November 1858, Bombay's official Oriental Translator climbed the steps of the Town Hall (now the Asiatic Society) to read to the assembled crowd the proclamation issued by Queen

Victoria taking over charge of India from the East India Company. As the territory became a possession of the Crown, Victoria promised 'to stimulate the peaceful industry of India, to promote works of public utility and improvement, and to administer its government for the benefit of all our subjects resident therein'. The artillery fired a salute and the Union Jack was hoisted, eliciting a murmur of alarm from the audience. The flag, it turned out, was upside down.

Though some believed that this was an ill omen, Bombay was headed for its most exuberant times. In 1861, the outbreak of the American Civil War left Britain bereft of the cotton its mills usually obtained from the plantations of the US South. India stepped into the breach, shipping much of its crop through Bombay port. Over the next five years, the value of Indian cotton exports to the UK jumped from Rs 16 crore to Rs 40 crore, as the price of Indian cotton rose from around four pence a pound in the Liverpool market to between twenty pence and twenty-four pence. 'King Cotton was the great deity at whose shrine...the merchant and the trader, the rich and the poor, high and low, master and servant, all paid pooja', wrote the Parsi politician Dinshaw Wacha, who had a ringside view of the unfolding events as a young trainee in the Bank of Bombay. Lancashire's demand for cotton was so great, he said, that 'even old mattresses were put into requisition to get the cotton, new beds being made of coir fibre'.

With so much money pouring in, the prices of everything soared—food, rents and wages. People on fixed salaries struggled under the pressure, but merchants couldn't find enough vehicles to invest in. In a script that would be repeated in the 1990s, scores of enterprises sprouted to accept their money. Banks and financial associations proliferated. So too did land and reclamation companies, known as khada. On the face of it, this seemed to make sense. It was evident that the island needed more room. The population, which had stood at 236,000 in 1836, had burgeoned to 816,562 in 1862. The Fort, one newspaper grumbled, looked like 'a large basket stuffed so full of goods that they threatened to fall out of it'. There were homes to be built, as also wharves, railway sheds and factories. Though previous reclamation projects had been planned by the government, Bombay's new governor, Bartle Frere, supported private participation in the activity. Of the paid-up capital of all companies registered between 1861 and 1863, reclamation companies accounted for just over 94 per cent. About £6 million of Bombay's cotton fortunes would be 'devoted to regulating and advancing...the whole of the island's foreshore' into the sea, said the official *Gazetteer*. Hills on the eastern ridge were levelled to provide filling for reclamation projects. Bombay's topography was completely altered. Its surface area expanded from twenty-nine square kilometres to thirty-five square kilometres.

But in the pursuit of easy profit, the reclamation

companies contributed to a speculative bubble. There was, as is so often the case, little relation between share prices and company earnings. Laying the basis for disaster were triangulated concerns—banks, financial associations and reclamation companies that had the same board of directors. Each entity worked to drive up the stock prices of its sister concerns, until shares were selling at absurd premiums. Promoters also formed groups to manipulate the market, whipping Bombay into a 'share mania'. Everyone, noted the Chamber of Commerce, 'from the highest to the lowest officials, merchants, adventurers, lawyers, editors, clerks and crossing sweepers' joined the speculative frenzy.

Of all the 'Share Kings', the most fabled figure was Premchand Roychand, whose exploits would help create another stereotype: he would be the first of many famous Bombayites who believed that profit held primacy over principle. 'No enchanter in Wonderland or Dreamland could have worked greater golden miracles by the magic of his consummate financial skill' than Roychand, wrote Dinshaw Wacha. The ingenious merchant was a promoter and shareholder in the Commercial Bank and Mercantile Bank, and associated with about seventy mushroom companies. He also took control of the Bank of Bombay. He had a sharp eye for the loophole and regulatory grey area. 'The other shareholders and directors allowed him to withdraw vast amounts of money from the Bank to finance his multitudinous schemes—directly and indirectly Rs 1.38 crores', a sum

Wacha described as 'a colossal and unheard of advance'. It was about half the Bank of Bombay's total capital. Inevitably, when news about the end of the American Civil War got around in March 1865, the price of cotton fell from twenty pence to ten pence in Liverpool. The next month it was even lower. On 1 July, hundreds of forward trades in Bombay matured, but few speculators had the cash to honour them. The city crashed 'with all the titanic force and velocity of an avalanche', Wacha recalled. Established banks and recent start-ups were all swept away, bankrupting thousands of people, rich and poor. 'It was a day when there hung a kind of funeral pall over the city', Wacha noted.

Roychand became the most hated man in Bombay— though not for long. If there's one thing Bombayites know him for today, it's the sentimental story of how, before his fall, he funded a clock tower at the University building with a carillon that chimed out the hours of the day. He did this, the legend goes, so that his mother, Rajabai, who was losing her sight, could keep track of the time and eat her dinner before sunset, as required by the conventions of Jainism. Since his death, Roychand's descendants have supported two biographies of the merchant, and in 2002, they funded a state-of-the-art exhibition hall in Bombay's main museum. At the inauguration, his great-grandson told *The Times of India* that the family had supported the Premchand Roychand Gallery because of their desire to 'recalibrate [the] focus' on their ancestor.

÷

Despite the magnitude of the disaster, Bombay managed to bounce back quicker than expected. By 1872, Bombay was the second-largest city in the Empire. The opening of the Suez Canal in 1869 helped revive trade by cutting the travel time from Bombay to Europe to a two-week journey. The recovery was also aided by the diversification some traders had made into manufacturing. In 1854, the Parsi merchant Cowasjee Nanabhai Davar had opened an establishment in Tardeo that left the writer Govind Narayan rapturous.

'The structure is about 400 hands long and about as broad', he wrote. 'It is full of machines and wheels which are whirring incessantly. Men are not required to power these wheels, which are whirring incessantly... These machines can produce in one day what a man needs 50 years to do.' The magical machines at the Bombay Spinning and Weaving Company were an attempt to fight Manchester and Lancashire with their own weapons, taking advantage of Bombay's access to cheap cotton and labour. Davar was so encouraged by the success of this factory that he opened the Bombay Throstle Mill shortly after.

By the early 1892, the city would have sixty-eight mills, employing 65,087 workers. In contrast to the pattern in other colonial cities, these enterprises were started with Indian capital and often run by Indian technicians. Migrants poured in to staff the factories, an overwhelming number of them Marathi-speaking men from the Konkan coastal strip south of Bombay, but also from the United Provinces in the north and other regions. That year, less than a quarter of Bombay's population had actually been born in the city. The mill workers would form a potent social and political force that would influence Bombay life for just under a century. They'd begun to stake their claim to their rights early on. India's first trade union, the Bombay Mill Hands Association, had been formed in 1884 to demand reasonable work hours, a weekly holiday and compensation for injuries sustained in factories.

In time, the male-dominated mill district, located a respectable distance away from the fashionable southern neighbourhoods, would develop a cultural life that amalgamated forms drawn from the breadth of Maharashtra and further afield. The processions that accompanied the Muslim observance of Muharram, for instance, which commemorates the martyrdom of the Prophet's grandson, Hussein, were joined by Maratha mill workers, who knew the occasion as Imam Jayanti—the Imam's birth anniversary. Before long, the mill district would be transformed from a mere geographical area into a 'locality', the resonant word Bombayites use to refer to the web of relationships and institutions that makes a place home. Emphasizing the uniqueness of their locality, textile workers, 90 per cent of whom lived within a fifteen-minute walk of their factories, began calling their swathe of the city Girangaon—the Village of Mills.

FIVE

Among the truths Bombay holds to be self-evident is the fact that it is cosmopolitan. The first time the word appeared in *The Times of India* in the context of the city was in 1878, in an article about Afghans visiting Bombay. The paper noted that groups of these men from the north, of whom 'nothing is finer than their physique, nothing worse than their morals', could frequently be spotted in 'the cosmopolitan bazaars of Bombay'. To inspect the roots of that heterogeneity, it's instructive to walk among the tombs of the dead in a neighbourhood that's recently come to be known as Wadala East. Just over a decade ago, it was called Antop Hill, a gritty industrial zone with gigantic storage tanks belonging to the Indian Oil Corporation and the factories of India Steel and India Hume Pipe Company. Antop Hill began to change early in the new millennium, a process driven in no small part by the construction of the Dosti Acres housing complex, where flats sell for around Rs 22,000 a square foot. But before the factories and the residential towers, Antop Hill was a necropolis. Since 1872, the neighbourhood has housed a burial ground for Sunni Muslims, a crematorium for Hindus and another, not so far away, for leprosy patients. It is also where the city's smallest communities have been allotted graveyards: the Armenians, the Chinese, the

Baha'is, the Prarthana Samaj and the Jews—or to be precise, Jewish prostitutes.

These cemeteries are the result of a tectonic shift that occurred shortly after the share mania of the 1860s. As the population burgeoned, the authorities decided to tear down the walls of the Fort to give the city room to expand. The plan was largely welcomed. 'Verily, the walls never did anything, nor protected anybody or anything except the city from ventilation and the breezes of the Konkan', one supporter of the project wrote. Today, only a single bastion of the old walls remains, on the edges of St George Hospital, near CST station. Despite this, the phantom presence of the citadel continues to be invoked every working day when millions of men and women march into the central business district that is still known as Fort. Many of them would have surged out of a railway station named for one of the old portals: Churchgate. Over the course of the day, some will attend to business in Bazaar Gate or grab lunch at one of the restaurants on Rampart Row. Lost from memory, however, are the series of tiny sally gates that town dwellers could crouch through in the night, after the main entry points had shut. A sentry would greet them with the cry, 'Ho kum dore'—a corruption of the question, 'Who comes there?' The traveller could proceed safely home to bed by offering the response, 'Friend'.

Bombay emerged from the wreckage of the stock market collapse chastened but wiser. With the demolition of the walls, the city 'threw out her arms like a giant refreshed in a new atmosphere and, Samson-wise, burst away from the bonds of a hundred years', wrote one supporter of the project. Some of the land freed up by the razing was sold to finance impressive public buildings. Several of these structures, like the High Court, would be built in the ponderous Gothic Revival style. Others, such as the postal headquarters, would pioneer the Indo-Saracenic style, which annotated the architectural fashions of Victorian Britain with Mughal domes, Bijapuri archways and Gujarati brackets.

Many marvels were emerging. In October 1866, gas lights began to illuminate parts of the city which, until then, had made do with the flicker of coconut oil lamps. In Byculla, an Agri-Horticultural Garden was being laid out, with a museum in its compound. A corona of handsome buildings was being constructed at Elphinstone Circle (now Horniman Circle), which had taken the place of the old Cotton Green. Plans were made to build more drains, especially after a dramatic rise in the number of deaths from cholera.

As the giant stretched its arms, seventy burial grounds came to be marooned in the middle of densely populated neighbourhoods and were deemed to be a public health hazard. In 1865, a Burial Commission suggested that all cemeteries within the city should be relocated. New graveyards were designated on Haines Road in Worli, in Sewri and other remote locations. Antop Hill, back of the beyond, became the final resting place for the tiniest ethnic groups.

In death, the occupants of the Antop Hill cemeteries are packed together more cosily with other members of their communities than they had been in life. Though people in the same profession or belonging to the same ethnic group tended to converge on the same neighbourhoods in Bombay, as they did in other large cities around the world, these enclaves were rather porous. The city had always been thrown together too tightly for rigid boundaries to endure. For the most, housing colonies that restricted ownership to members of specific religious groups had renters from other communities. Bungalows in affluent parts of town had smaller structures in the back for domestic workers or entire pockets of homes for the service staff. Significantly, the edges of most neighbourhoods were fuzzy, leaving intermediate zones in which no particular group was dominant.

Of all the groups buried on Antop Hill, only the Chinese had their own residential cluster—a single lane near the docks in Mazagaon they shared with Parsi, Catholic and Maharashtrian neighbours. On Chinese New Year, some of the 5,500 members of the community still gather outside the Kwan Tai Shek temple in the area to light crackers and perform dragon dances. The earliest Chinese settlers had arrived in Bombay around 1850 to work at a factory the Parsi merchant Framjee Cawasjee had opened in Powai to manufacture silk, tea and sugar. Other Chinese people found employment as carpenters in the docks. Their graves, relocated to Antop Hill from Shuklaji Street in Byculla, are testimony to their ability to retain a sense of identity in an environment that has occasionally been overtly hostile, and to adapt to their changing circumstances. While the older gravestones bear inscriptions in Chinese, the newer ones are in English. Over the decades, fewer community members have learned how to write the old script, and sculptors with the ability to engrave these on the tombs have vanished.

The Armenians, whose ancestors came to India as traders, have lived in Bombay since 1676, when they were offered concessions by the East India Company to settle in the islands. At first, they buried their dead in the compound of a home in Byculla, but in 1813 were moved to a burial ground in Girgaum. Many Armenian graves in the Antop Hill cemetery are marked by crosses decorated with vines, a motif that symbolizes regeneration—a state of grace that is sadly beyond the community's grasp. In 1983, with their numbers dwindling, the Armenians allowed the Baha'i community to share their cemetery, just as they would later grant Bombay's Syrian Christians use of their ancient church on Medows Street in the Fort. Today, there's only one Armenian left in the city, Zabel Joshi née Hayakian, who found a home in Bombay after she married a city businessman she met in Beirut.

The Baha'is were allotted space on Antop Hill in 1905, just twelve years after the death of the founder of their faith, Baha'u'llah, in Akká in present-day Israel. Bombay has always had a close association with the young faith. Baha'u'llah's son, Mirza Muhammad Ali, travelled here in the early 1880s to supervise the publication of his father's texts. Baha'i texts teach that cemeteries must look like a gulistan ('garden' in Persian), so floral motifs are common on the Antop Hill graves. Flower plants fill the plot, a burst of serenity in the concrete-laden neighbourhood.

Next to the Armenians and Baha'is lie members of the Prarthana Samaj, the Maharashtrian sibling of the Brahmo Samaj reform movement started by Raja Ram Mohan Roy in Bengal only two decades before the Antop Hill cemeteries were opened. The men and women who rest here were passionately involved in India's intellectual life. Narayan Chandavarkar, for instance, served as president of the Indian National Congress in 1900. Near him is the grave of Balwant Nagarkar, who accompanied Swami Vivekananda to a meeting of the World Parliament of Religions in Chicago in 1893. Reflecting a very Bombay desire to be modern without completely discarding tradition, the Prarthana Samaj devised its own death rituals, cremating members and then burying their ashes. That was entirely in keeping with the vision of the Prarthana Samaj pioneer, M. G. Ranade. 'The dead and the buried are dead, buried and burnt once for all, and the dead past cannot, therefore, be revived except by a reformation of the old materials into new organised beings', he had written.

The most intriguing of all the graveyards doesn't exist anymore. The burial ground for Jewish prostitutes was first encroached by slum dwellers and then requisitioned for a transportation project. It started operations in 1869, the year the Suez Canal was inaugurated. Trade and passenger traffic to India grew significantly. But the establishment of regular steamer communication, a book on the Bombay police complained later, brought 'the riff-raff of Europe' to the city. 'Before the opening of the Suez Canal... the foreign prostitute from Eastern Europe was practically unknown in Bombay and such immorality as it existed was confined to women of Eurasian or Indian parentage', the book said. So many Eastern European women found their way to the Kamathipura red light district that Cursetji Shuklaji Street, where they settled, came to be known as safed gully or white lane. (Japanese women also had their own quarter in the neighbourhood, but they mainly entertained their compatriots. Some of them lie in a plot on Haines Road in Worli.) Though there's no trace of the Jewish prostitutes' graveyard, the classified ads in today's tabloids make it clear that the charms of women from Eastern Europe still hold considerable appeal in Bombay.

÷

Despite the attractions of the Eastern European ladies and their Indian counterparts, Bombay's greatest pleasures in the nineteenth century were taken in public. Every evening, groups of men 'ate the air' on the maidan—the vast fields on the seaward side of the Fort walls that had been kept open to ensure a clear range of fire in the event of an invasion. The men formed 'mat and lantern clubs', so designated because of the apparatus they bore with them. The members would sit around the dim light to play noisy games of cards, chess and chowpat. Vendors wandered between the groups selling cubes of sugarcane, calling, 'Ganderi, goolab ganderi.' Sometimes, Parsi priests would regale the crowds with stories of Persian heroes such as Jamshed, or Rustam and Sorab. Most often, the men would disperse at 8 p.m. to eat dinner at home, but sometimes, each of them would bring their meal with them. 'The members ate together a repast which, if not luxurious, was at least rich in the embarrassing variety of dishes', one participant recalled. 'The pungent bhajia chatni and the sweet sugarcane pieces bought off hawkers served as delicacies to the miscellaneous meal.'

On festival days, the maidan hosted fairs at which English and Swiss mechanical toys were greatly sought after. A doll that could say 'mama' sold for Rs 5. Further south, crowds sat on benches around the Bandstand at 5 p.m. two or three times a week to listen to performances by the Governor's band. When the band wasn't playing, the area was 'quite overrun with children and ayahs' of all races and religions, reported D. Aubrey in a series of letters to his friends in England in 1883.

As darkness fell, the action moved to Apollo Bunder,

'the resort...of the European and Oriental fashionable world'. This is how Aubrey described the perfervid scene: 'Here the exquisites, beaux and dandies of two civilizations have already congregated. British belles are lounging over the sides of their victorias to chatter with their husbands or inamoratas, whilst the rich Parsee lady, clad in silken garments, reclines in the back of her carriage... With tremendous éclat, a few jovial trios of sportive Mohammedans dash past in swaying dog-carts'.

When they were done with their promenading, Bombayites consumed—and created—culture of all sorts. There were tamasha artists and acrobats, snake charmers and rope dancers. Winter brought European circus troupes, opera companies and American minstrelsy performers. Bombay's streets and music rooms resounded with rhythms as varied as its citizenry. There was plenty of popular entertainment to be found, of course, but as the nineteenth century progressed, Bombay became an important centre for art music too. With royal courts crumbling in the face of expanding British power, performers were deprived of traditional sources of patronage; Bombay's merchant princes filled the gap. Giants of the music world, from both north and south, began to frequent the city. Many made Bombay their home.

Among them were three brothers from Bijnaur in Uttar Pradesh—Nazir, Chhaju and Khadim Hussain Khan, who had spent decades studying with great ustads around India. When they arrived in Bombay around 1870, they set up home in Bhendi Bazaar, a commercial neighbourhood in the Native Town within walking distance of the Grant Road theatre district and the pleasure houses of Kamathipura. They were soon absorbed into Bombay's musical networks and were sought-after performers. Nazir Khan, especially, won acclaim for his exacting breath control and sonorous voice. They also earned respect for their scholarship. The brothers had an enviable grasp of the nuances of hundreds of compositions, and began to collaborate with the musicologist V. N. Bhatkhande in his ambitious endeavour to catalogue north Indian music.

Not surprisingly, the energy of their adopted city began to find expression in their music. The Khans developed a style characterized by slow, open-throated singing and an improvizational technique that used only a limited number of notes. It remains Bombay's only home-grown classical music tradition and is still known as the Bhendi Bazaar gharana.

When the Khan sahibs weren't mentoring students at home in Bhendi Bazaar, they conducted classes at the Parsi Gayan Uttejak Mandali, a music society established by K. N. Kabraji, the energetic editor of a reformist newspaper called *Rast Goftar* (Truth Teller). A man of eclectic interests, like so many Bombayites of his era, Kabraji was crazy about cricket, women's education, drama and music. He set up the Mandali in 1870 'to propagate among Parsis a liking for indigenous music and promote songs which are moral'.

Despite its high-minded intentions, the Mandali proved rather scandalous. In an age in which it was taboo for respectable people to sing in public, it encouraged its middle-class members to perform at its biweekly concerts. Even more radical was the Mandali's inclusion in its shows of items by the daughters of some members. The first time Parsi girls sang in public, in 1876, there was an uproar. One newspaper suggested that the students had been forced to sing objectionable songs. Kabraji filed a libel suit against the writer (and won).

It wasn't just the performers at the Mandali's concerts that defied convention—the structure of the performances did too. Departing from the tradition of featuring only a few compositions at each performance, the Mandali's jalsas were sometimes packed with up to thirty-six items, a novelty that Kabraji and other members may have adopted after attending the concerts of Western classical music that were becoming increasingly frequent in Bombay. The Parsi Gayan Uttejak Mandali's engagement with the numerous Western forms swirling around them in nineteenth-century Bombay was made explicit on 21 March 1887, when members performed a concert at the Town Hall in a style that has since been recognized as 'fusion'. The programme included a Negro Minstrelsy tune (sung in Burmese), a khayal (accompanied by the piano) and a choral rendition of Raga Jhinjhoti (backed by the organ master of St Thomas Cathedral). The evening ended with a fifty-voice chorus singing *Raksh Dev Tu Maharani*—a Gujarati translation of *God Save the Queen*.

The concert was a particularly vigorous display of Kabraji's polyglot sensibilities, but by now, his mix-and-match aesthetic was already gaining fans around the subcontinent. A decade before the Town Hall concert, Kabraji had founded the Victoria Theatrical Company, which mounted performances in the entertainment quarter at Grant Road. (The neighbourhood is still referred to as Pila House, a mangled recollection of the Play House that had been inaugurated in 1846.) On the stages of Grant Road, with colourful backdrops illuminated by gas lamps, amateur and professional groups presented a range of plays: tales from the epics, both Hindu and Parsi; productions of Shakespeare in Gujarati and Marathi; and farces that satirized social foibles in the hope of effecting reform. Kabraji was a skilled playwright himself, finding inspiration in Firdausi's *Shahnama*, Sheridan's *The School for Scandal* and the controversies of the day (his works included *The Cleanliness of City Dwellers vs The Simplicity of Villagers*). The productions, like the city that was watching them, frequently slipped between languages, and mashed together a variety of performance forms.

Kabraji was among the first to identify the business potential of these entertainments. Merchant princes began to invest in Bombay's theatre companies and send them off on countrywide tours. For more than half a century, groups like Kabraji's Victoria travelled through India with productions that blended themes, narrative techniques and musical styles drawn from the subcontinent, the Middle East and Europe. Acknowledging the roots of the men who created India's first commercial theatre circuit, the form came to be known as Parsi Theatre. But though the financiers and managers were Parsi, the actors, playwrights and stagehands represented the entire spectrum of Bombay's religious and ethnic groups. India was enthralled by their enactments of cosmopolitanism.

Despite these displays of stage perfection, however, life on the streets was occasionally discordant. Riots between Parsis and Muslims broke out in 1874 after a Parsi publication carried an article that criticized Islam, accompanied by a caricature of the Prophet. In 1893, against the backdrop of a high-pitched campaign against cow-slaughter, skirmishes between Hindus and Muslims left eighty people dead. Eerily, the violence occurred in many of the neighbourhoods that would become conflict zones in religious riots exactly a century later. But in the 1890s, Bombay had a rich experience of random interactions in public spaces and a sophisticated web of institutions to help it draw itself together again.

SIX

His first visit to Bombay was not a particularly happy one. He'd arrived from Rajkot on 11 August 1888, and expected to spend ten days in the city before his ship sailed for England, where he was going to study law. But the sea was rough and his brother, fearful of a mishap, asked him to postpone his voyage. As he waited for clement weather, he was summoned to a meeting of members of his caste and informed by the headman of the Modh Banias that their religion forbade voyages abroad. When the oceans finally calmed on 4 September, Mohandas Karamchand Gandhi was relieved to leave the city.

But over the course of his peripatetic life, Bombay would be the closest thing he would know to home in India. The man who believed that India's future lay in its villages had a complex emotional relationship with Bombay. He spent seventeen years in Mani Bhavan in Gamdevi, but before that had homes in Girgaum and in Santa Cruz. The city he called 'the hope of my dreams' was the testing ground for many of his ideas and the place where he announced his key strategies: satyagraha, non-cooperation, swadeshi and prohibition (which Bombay wasn't very keen about).

The most powerful idea of the future that Bombay created for India, it's clear, was the dream of freedom.

For many, the journey from the village to the city was the opportunity to re-imagine the sometimes stifling ties of caste and community. In India's most modern city, villagers who had drawn their sense of self from a collective discovered the courage to become individuals—or at least, to become as individualistic as possible in a place where, a Census report observed, 'a dozen families herd together in houses only large enough to contain one'.

Though Bombay had sat out the 1857 uprising, it would, three decades later, become the beating heart of India's struggle for political freedom. Gandhi would be the central figure in that battle, but it had started three years before his first visit to Bombay. At noon on 28 December 1885, a group of seventy-two men gathered in Gokuldas Tejpal Sanskrit College on the banks of Gowalia Tank for the first session of the Indian National Congress. Bombay sent the largest contingent of delegates—seventeen lawyers, teachers and editors who reflected the energetic participation of the city's professional classes in India's most important debates. To be sure, their proposals were modest. The Congress aimed to promote friendship among those working for India's cause and to consolidate a sense of national unity. But it would soon grow more insistent and stir the subcontinent to action.

The Gandhi era dawned in Bombay in 1915, when the lawyer returned to India after twenty-one years in South Africa. He was given a rapturous welcome as he disembarked in the city, but he still wasn't able to warm to it. 'I don't like Bombay', he told a nephew. 'I see here all the shortcomings of London but find none of its amenities.' The Mahatma, ever sensitive to suffering, was well aware of the strained conditions in which the city's workers lived. A few years later, he noted, 'Bombay is beautiful, not for its big buildings, for most of them hide squalid poverty and dirt, not for its wealth, for most of it has been derived from the blood of the masses, but for its generosity'.

That magnanimity cut across class lines. Each time Gandhi called for donations, it wasn't only sympathetic industrialists and traders who opened their purses— large numbers of common folk would also offer cash or even family jewellery. Even though a Census report noted that most Bombay residents lived on starvation diets, the city ensured that Gandhi's movement never ran out of funds. That took some effort, for as the Congress leader Sarojini Naidu is said to have observed, 'It costs a lot of money to keep the Mahatma in poverty'.

In 1919, Gandhi had his first opportunity to demonstrate the power of the passive resistance techniques he'd experimented with in South Africa. With the passage of the Rowlatt Act granting provincial governments sweeping powers to quash dissent, Gandhi announced a day of protest and self-purification on 6 April. Bombay participated eagerly. Thousands joined his twenty-four-hour fast. Women dressed in black marched in processions to Chowpatty to symbolize the nation's sorrow. Approximately 150,000 turned out for the meeting on the beach to pray that the Act would be repealed.

Over the next four decades, the thoroughfares and maidans on which Bombayites congregated to eat the air would become the theatres in which individuals belonging to diverse castes and religious groups discovered the glory of collective action. India's most materialistic city would find it in itself to start dressing in course homespun, give up liquor and repeatedly brave police lathis. Through Gandhi's example and cajoling, Bombay would understand the need for negotiation and compromise, and for taking the long view in light of the short-term setback.

Many of those lessons were learned during the Non-Cooperation Movement, launched in 1920. Among its cornerstones was the idea of swadeshi—self-reliance, with its attendant strategy of boycotting foreign goods. As was to be expected, the campaign, which had direct impact on Bombay's wallet, divided opinion in India's industrial capital. While mill workers and the Gujarati and Marwari traders in the city's cloth markets were keen supporters of the nationalist cause, mill owners, who often needed to import machinery, tended to be loyal to the British. Among the exceptions was Umar Sobani, the owner of Elphinstone Mill. On 31 July 1921, as 12,000 people gathered in the compound of his factory, Sobani stepped forward to set fire to a huge pile of foreign-made clothes. Volunteers had gone door to door collecting garments for the bonfire. By one account, the clothes tossed into the bonfire were worth Rs 30,000.

The bonfires were lit again on 17 November, the day that the Prince of Wales arrived in Bombay to tour the empire he would later inherit. Gandhi's followers wanted the flames to be high enough for the prince to see as he landed at Apollo Bunder, far across town. But the day ended in violence. When Congress cadres returning from the bonfire disembarked at Charni Road and Marine Lines stations, they found themselves in the midst of Parsis and Anglo-Indians going home after lining the route of the prince's welcome procession. The prince's supporters were attacked savagely, whereupon some of them retaliated with equal ferocity. Gandhi decided to go on a fast until peace was restored, but calm descended only five days later, by which time fifty people had been killed. Gandhi was distraught. He addressed a letter to the 'hooligans of Bombay', stating, 'It cuts me to the quick to find that you have used the mass awakening for your own lust for plunder, rapine and even indulging in your worse animal appetite'.

The nationalist movement would spread so rapidly, it would even hinder the land reclamation that seemed to proceed in Bombay of its own volition. Since 1873, about 165 acres of land had been reclaimed along the eastern coast between Colaba and Sewri, most of it being used to expand the docks and the railways. In 1905, a fashionable neighbourhood called Cuffe Parade began to be built on 89,360 square yards reclaimed on the western shore of Colaba. Ever since water had begun to be piped in from the Vihar and Tulsi lakes, the tanks and wells that had slaked the city's thirst were deemed health hazards and had gradually been filled over. Gowalia Tank, near the school at which the Congress had first met, was transformed into a maidan in 1911 and would, in a few decades, become the site for one of Gandhi's most significant announcements. In 1914, the Port Trust began to work on a twenty-two-acre project, using rocks and sand excavated for the new Alexandra Dock. When it was completed in 1918, the Ballard Estate business district would house the offices of the biggest shipping and commercial firms.

But, by the 1920s, having gradually forced the British to allow more Indians to be elected to the municipal council and the legislative council, the nationalists were in a position to keep a closer eye on the manner in which the reclamation projects were being conducted. In 1926, an associate of Gandhi named K. F. Nariman exposed the flawed assumptions on which the Back Bay Reclamation Scheme was being carried out. The project was intended to create 1,145 acres on the western shore to decongest the city, whose population had touched 1.1 million. Its logic was a little circuitous: the land would be allocated to rich people to build homes by the sea, leaving the areas of the city they vacated open for poor people.

Nariman hammered away at the government, first as

a member of the municipal corporation, and then in the legislative council. 'This mad and chimerical project has practically mortgaged the resources of the Presidency for at least a generation to come', he observed. In 1926, the municipality appointed a vigilance committee to supervise the project. Later, an inquiry committee began to consider Nariman's allegations of corruption and favouritism. This was a terrible embarrassment for the colonial government. Eventually, the project was scaled back—but not before a large portion of Padan Hill in Kandivali had been quarried and its load of stone-age tools piled on the Colaba foreshore. On those sections would be constructed buildings whose facades juxtaposed motifs of Babylonian ziggurats, Greek sunbursts and streamlined cow heads, giving the fashionable Art Deco style a very Bombay mien.

On 6 April 1930, Bombayites turned their attention to the shore again as Gandhi marched to Dandi in Gujarat to defy the government's monopoly on making salt. In the city, five men and two women had been chosen to break the salt law. They carried water from the sea and boiled it in vessels on the beach at Haji Ali. Salt pans were built on the terrace of Congress House, near Kennedy Bridge, and the mineral sold across the city to raise funds for the struggle. A few days later, more than a thousand men and women defied the police to march on the Wadala salt depot, not far from the multi-ethnic cemeteries. When news about Gandhi's arrest in Gujarat on 5 May reached Bombay, the markets shut down and a huge protest rally was held on the Esplanade. Six donkeys were paraded in foreign-made clothes.

The success of the Salt Satyagraha fuelled Bombay's demand for khadi. Wearing homespun—and spinning it—became a fashion statement even for the rich. In 1931, the Khadi Bhandar in Kalbadevi sold cloth worth Rs 7.4 lakh. Branches were set up in short order at Flora Fountain and as far afield as Vile Parle. Gandhi was zealous in his attempt to propagate the virtues of homespun. He even offered to give spinning lessons to Lady Lloyd, the wife of the governor who had been at the centre of the Back Bay scandal that Nariman had exposed.

The Civil Disobedience Movement was taking place against the backdrop of a huge spurt of unemployment and wage cuts in the wake of the Great Depression. Bombay's industrialists believed that the boycott of foreign goods and firms that used them would only deepen the recession by locking in scarce capital. By October 1930, twenty-four mills—a quarter of those in the city—had shut. Industrialists complained that the constant hartals were hurting the business climate. The movement was called off in March 1931 with the signing of the Gandhi-Irwin Pact, by which the British government withdrew restrictions on the activities of the Congress, but it wasn't until 1935 that the economy began to show signs of recovery. That year brought another sign of hope: the Government of India

Act, which allowed Indians to form governments in the provinces. On 19 July 1937, a Popular Ministry headed by B. G. Kher took charge of Bombay State and announced a budget designed to provide relief to rural areas. It abolished grazing fees, reduced land taxes for farmers and allocated funds for water supply schemes. The ministry also instituted a policy of prohibition. Delegations of Parsi liquor traders tried to persuade Gandhi to reverse the decision, as did groups of toddy-tapping Bhandaris, whose livelihoods would be lost. Even the Archbishop of Bombay wrote him a letter. But Gandhi was adamant. 'I am sure that the removal of the curse of intoxicating drinks will confer lasting benefits on the country', he maintained.

The complaints of the city's liquor traders and industrialists were relatively mild compared to some of the other criticism Gandhi faced in the city. As it turned out, two of the Mahatma's most spirited political opponents were Bombay men, who had honed their ideas and oratorical skills in the city's conference halls and at the rallies on its maidans.

For B. R. Ambedkar, Bombay and other cities were instruments of emancipation for the Depressed Classes whom he represented. He was an excellent example of this himself, a boy from an 'untouchable' caste who had been educated in Bombay's best high school and then made his way to Columbia University in New York. Ambedkar dismissed Gandhi's efforts to 'uplift' members of the lower castes as paternalistic. He believed that the caste system was intrinsic to Hinduism and that Dalits would find redemption only if they left the fold, a contention that Gandhi countered furiously in numerous columns and speeches.

Mohammed Ali Jinnah's disagreement with Gandhi's vision of India was even more fundamental. When Gandhi returned from South Africa, Jinnah had presided over a reception to welcome him home. The monocled Muslim lawyer was equally at home attending the dances at the Taj Mahal Hotel with his young wife, the Parsi heiress Ruttie, as he was making impassioned speeches at political meetings at Shantaram's Chawl in Girgaum. But in 1920, Jinnah left the Congress to head the Muslim League. He began to argue that Muslims and Hindus constituted distinct nationalities. In 1938, Gandhi and Jinnah had a series of meetings in Bombay to discuss their differing perspectives on the 'communal problem', the phrase commonly used to describe the issue. No compromise could be reached, but Gandhi remained cautiously optimistic. 'Every attempt must be made to arrive at a mutual understanding', he wrote. Gandhi was still mulling over strategies to win back Jinnah when, months after the Second World War was declared in 1939, the Popular Ministry resigned to express its opposition to India having been declared a belligerent without the consent of its citizens being sought. In the initial years of the conflict, the British took a mauling. In August 1942, as the Japanese seemed poised to invade India, Gandhi arrived in Bombay to address a meeting of the All India Congress Committee in Gowalia Maidan. The day before, he and his colleagues held a meeting to decide on an appropriate slogan to express their opposition to British rule. 'Get out', one suggested. Gandhi thought that too impolite. Another suggested 'Retreat' or 'Withdraw' but those didn't find approval either. Finally, Yusuf Meherally turned to Gandhi with a bow and said, 'Quit India'. Said Gandhi, 'Amen'.

By September 1945, when the Labour Party won the British elections, the road to freedom was cleared. More than 100,000 people returned to Gowalia Maidan to discuss forthcoming elections to the central and provincial legislatures, the foreign exchange balances that India had accumulated in England and other matters related to how free India would function. But Independence came at a price. In September 1944, Gandhi had strolled up Malabar Hill fourteen times to speak with Jinnah in his home on Mount Pleasant Road. Though they had appeared amiable enough when they smiled for the cameras at the end of their negotiations, Jinnah reiterated that the Muslim League would settle for nothing less than an independent state.

In February 1946, though the corpse of colonialism was already in the coffin, the sailors at the naval signals school, the *Talwar*, hammered in the final nail. The morning the navy chief was due to visit, they painted the slogan 'Quit India' on their ship and the walls of their barracks. The agitation soon spread to other vessels in the Bombay harbour; some of them unfurled the tricolour. On 21 February, a six-hour gun battle ensued as the sailors tried to capture the armoury in Bombay Castle, where Garcia da Orta had once lived, the kernel of the modern city of Bombay. Mill workers and other Bombay residents flooded into the streets to support the navy men. By the time a ceasefire was brokered by Congress leader Vallabhbhai Patel, 223 Bombay residents had died.

Freedom came amidst a shortage of milk and sugar as Bombay devoured piles of celebratory sweets. At midnight on 15 August 1947, B. G. Kher, who had resumed his position as head of the provincial ministry, raised the tricolour over the secretariat and declared, 'Citizens of free India—you are now free'. After a shastri, a moulvi, a Catholic bishop and a Parsi priest said appropriate prayers, Kher touched a switch and the buildings behind him burst into light. A mighty roar went up and brass bands blared out raucous tunes. A river of revellers swept through the streets, waving tricolours, riding in trams and on top of them. While Delhi and Calcutta were wrenched apart by riots sparked by the anxieties of Partition, Bombay was peaceful and joyous. Reported *The Times of India*, 'Hundreds of thousands marched cheering through the illuminated streets of Bombay, uninterruptedly shouting slogans in a multitude of tongues, which turned the city at midnight into a Babel'.

As India journeyed to independence, Gandhi had

fundamentally reshaped Bombay. Gandhi had helped the city understand that reform wasn't a process effected merely by institutions or governments—it demanded individual responsibility and effort. Bombay had also learned that achieving real change required the participation of people across class, caste and religious lines. During the freedom movement, Bombay had, despite its babel of tongues and visions, found a way to agree on a singular purpose.

On 28 February 1948, a month after Gandhi had fallen to an assassin's bullet in Delhi, the men of the First Battalion of the Somerset Light Infantry marched under the Gateway of India to board *The Empress of Australia,* ending the British presence in India. The islands their countrymen had acquired 282 years earlier were unrecognizable. So too were the people who had come to inhabit them.

PART TWO

ONE

The last time I'd visited Bharat Nagar, it had been a little inconvenient to get to. Located on a spit of land protruding into the mouth of the Mithi river, the Muslim-dominated settlement had only one swampy road running through it—and that road had been blocked by the skeleton of a bus that had been set afire by about fifty young men, protesting the demolition of the Babri Masjid in Ayodhya the previous evening. As the bus went up in flames, policemen shot at the protestors with pistols, .303 rifles and Sten guns. A little while later, hundreds of people surrounded the police outpost at the tip of the slum, hurling stones and tube lights that left holes in the corrugated asbestos roof. The four men on duty attempted to fight their way out, killing three attackers and wounding fifty-four. When I got there in a *Times of India* jeep a few hours later on the evening of 7 December 1992, the road was littered with shards of metal and glass.

Twenty years after the violence, everything seemed so unfamiliar, I couldn't even locate the police chowki. I realized that it had shifted into a solid building down the road and its place had been taken by a barber's shop, run by a man named Shaikh Mansoor. It was a slow day, so Mansoor offered to walk me around the neighbourhood. We wandered past Ambika Jewellers,

Stallion the Design Master and Zaika—Chinese Mughlai and Sea Food. Mansoor was fourteen when the riots broke out and he had watched the attack on the police post from behind the wall of a neighbour's home. 'The guns sounded like thunder,' he recalled. Much had changed in the two decades since the dangal. The flimsy metal-sheeted shanties had been replaced by brick structures, he pointed out, and the tidal pools had disappeared because the Mithi river was now held back by thick concrete walls.

But the changes in his slum colony, Mansoor observed, were nowhere as dramatic as the transformations across the street—a six-lane road that didn't even exist at the time of the riots. Since 1992, a 370-hectare business district called the Bandra Kurla Complex had been reclaimed from the creek that once surrounded Bharat Nagar. The glass-fronted National Stock Exchange now looms over Mansoor's settlement, while the US Consulate and a branch of the Michelin-starred restaurant Yauatcha are a short walk away. Also in the vicinity is the head office of the Securities and Exchange Bureau of India, an institution that was established months before the riots in 1992, to regulate the recently liberalized financial markets. Less than two weeks after it had been constituted, it was called on to investigate a \$920-million stock market swindle executed by a young trader named Harshad Mehta. Like Premchand Roychand, Mehta was a master at squeezing through the loophole and like Roychand, he was lionized—until thousands lost their savings when the market crashed.

The Bandra Kurla Complex isn't the only reclamation project undertaken in the city since the riots. A study conducted by the Mumbai University's geography department in 2012 used satellite imagery and remote sensing technologies to detect 54.7 square kilometres of land that has been created since 1990. The images showed substantial reclamation near Bhandup and around Manori Creek, while mudflats in Gorai and Mahul have been built over. But the largest reclamations, the researchers noted, were in Malad, where an office complex called Mindspace has been constructed atop a 19.2-hectare coastal garbage dump. Where Bombay once had to quarry hills to expand, it is currently rising on its own waste. Several call centres located in the Malad complex have reported that their computers are given to frequent malfunctions. Evidently, the sulphuric fumes from the rubbish tip underneath are corroding the machines.

A great deal of the recent reclamation—or 'anthropogenic structural interventions', as the experts describe them—is illegal. The photographs taken from outer space couldn't identify who had occupied this land, but the environmental consequences could be disastrous. The researchers said that most of this new land is in the intertidal zone, which is classified as being ecologically sensitive. Reclamations have stripped the city of 40 per cent of its mangrove cover in the decade since 1995, depriving Bombayites of a natural flood barrier and silt trap.

Alongside these reclamations, Bombay is experiencing another, more unsettling process: the emergence of new islands, whose edges are sharply defined by religion and class. As it turns out, the riots and the retaliatory bomb blasts that followed them coincided with the beginnings of India's policy of economic liberalization. Both events unleashed forces that have profoundly reorganized Bombay's landscape. They have created enclaves of privilege and exclusion that undermine Bombay's deep-seated idea of itself as a progressive, cosmopolitan metropolis.

÷

In the end, the most vivid image I would retain would be that of sweaty men from Shivaji Park pushing their cars off the beach at Dadar at dawn, looking embarrassed but defiant. They'd heard that Iranian commandos were speeding across the Arabian Sea to join forces with Bombay's Muslims, so night after night, they'd drive to the shore and shine their headlights on the dark bay, prepared to repel the invaders with hockey sticks and cricket stumps. By the morning, their car batteries would be drained, so they'd have to shove their Fiats off the sand, exhausted from their vigil but proud that they'd done their bit to safeguard their city.

That was only one of the many surreal events that would occur in Bombay in the months after

6 December 1992, the day that the Babri Masjid
in distant Ayodhya was demolished by Hindu
fundamentalists. That afternoon, tens of thousands of
supporters of the Bharatiya Janata Party broke through
steel barricades around the mosque they claimed had
been built over the birthplace of the god Ram. In a few
hours, they destroyed the ancient structure and severely
damaged India's idea of itself as a secular nation. It
was the culmination of a corrosive campaign led by a
man perched on a Toyota mini-bus fitted out to look
like a medieval chariot. When he set out in 1990, L. K.
Advani, the leader of the Bharatiya Janata Party, had
left a trail of violence across north India, but Bombay
was, of course, immune to those atavistic passions. It
was, we all knew, India's most cosmopolitan city, an
oasis of amity whose only business was business.

The morning after the mosque was torn down, I
got off at Sandhurst Road station to stroll down to
the predominantly Muslim quarter of Bhendi Bazaar
to gather some opinions for the reaction story that
the paper would no doubt be putting together that
evening. I expected to encounter profound anger, but
when I turned on to Mohammed Ali Road, I found
myself in a war zone. Barricades had materialized at
every junction, constructed from metal tree guards, an
uprooted bus stand, even someone's old dressing table.

Youths with swords and daggers ran through the
bylanes. The dull thud of police .303 rifles could be
heard everywhere. On Shaukat Ali Road, I met the

family of Naseem Khan, who lived in a tiny second-floor flat just past a police guard post. A bullet had pierced her head as she'd bent over a clothesline in the balcony to fetch a napkin for her mother-in-law. At JJ Hospital nearby, I watched injured people being rushed in on handcarts and cars, hawkers' trolleys and ambulances. Twelve operation theatres had been set up. A battery of nurses worked feverishly, cutting gauze for bandages. One orderly was simply trying to keep the floor from getting excessively blood-splattered. Three hours after the police had first opened fire, nine bodies were piled up in a stairwell by the entrance, not so far away from the statue of the patron. By the evening, forty-three people across the city would be dead and ninety-three injured, seventy of them falling to police bullets.

Over the next few days, I'd travel to parts of Bombay I'd only been dimly aware of: Pascal Colony in Jogeshwari, Bainganwadi in Deonar, and Asalpha village in Ghatkopar. One afternoon, I sat on the water tank on top of one of the few tall buildings in Dharavi watching dozens of skirmishes proceeding across the shantytown. Groups of men separated only by a drainage canal or a boundary wall were hurling Molotov cocktails at each other. The injured were being carried through the gullies on makeshift stretchers.

Even though the army was rumbling through the streets in Shaktiman trucks to assist the police, it took three days for the violence to dissipate. The riots would leave 202 people dead, 130 of them Muslim. The vast majority of the Muslim dead—ninety-eight—had fallen to police bullets. Compensation packages were announced for the victims and everyone was relieved that the worst had passed, though baffled about why the violence had broken out in the first place. Soon, the newspapers were running ads for Christmas and New Year's dinner-dances.

Three weeks later, on 6 January 1993, traffic outside Masjid station was blocked by a sea of white-capped mathadi workers, who made their living as loaders in the city's docks and warehouses. Two of their fraternity had been murdered the night before and they'd called a bandh in protest. Their leaders believed that the crime had been committed by members of a rival union and they took care to emphasize that the incident was not motivated by religious hatred. But the match had been struck.

The next afternoon, the barricades had reappeared in Bhendi Bazaar. On Shaukat Ali Road, just past the home of Naseem Khan, the housewife killed by the stray bullet, I found myself on the edges of a mob that had fixed their sights on a taxi driver who had pulled up to use a public toilet on the corner. They forced him to open his fly. He wasn't circumcised. Blood spurted from his abdomen as he ran down the street to collapse in a heap by a blue police van fifty metres away. 'He's bleeding like a pigeon with its neck twisted off,' one young attacker gloated as the policemen helped the driver into their vehicle. Nine taxi drivers who found themselves in the wrong neighbourhoods would be attacked that evening.

Just past midnight, the gruesome burning of six members of a Hindu family in Jogeshwari would provide the excuse for an unimaginably vicious attack to be launched against the lives and livelihoods of Bombay's Muslims. An exaggerated version of the 'Radhabai Chawl incident', as it came to be known, was published on the front page of *Saamna,* the paper of the chauvinistic Shiv Sena party. 'Fourteen defenceless citizens were burnt alive by traitorous fanatics', it said. 'Even if the government is wearing a green burkha and standing on a street corner of Bhendi Bazaar with bangles in hand, lakhs of Hindu youths will keep this nation alive... If there's no wound on the body, a victory is meaningless. The next few days will be ours.'

At that signal, Sena cadres stepped out of the party's 221 street-corner shakhas. Every Muslim was a target. Residents of buildings from affluent Malabar Hill to middle-class Borivali scrambled to unscrew the nameplates on their doors and in their lobbies, hoping to confuse potential attackers. The *Times* newsroom was flooded with calls from frantic Muslims telling us that they could see mobs approaching and that the police were refusing to provide protection. 'If you call, perhaps they'll listen,' the callers would beg.

Ragtag vigilante armies patrolled the streets (and Dadar beach) each night to defend their neighbourhoods. Approximately 100,000 Muslims became refugees in their own city, seeking shelter in rudimentary relief camps set up in safe neighbourhoods. The railway stations were crowded with people, both Muslim and Hindu, fleeing Bombay: the violence had deprived daily wage earners of work. An estimated 150,000 people would leave on special trains bound for Bihar and Uttar Pradesh.

It would later emerge that the Sainiks had accessed municipal records to find out where Muslims lived and which businesses they owned. Large stores such as the vehicle dealer Allibhai Premji and furniture maker Noormohammed's were incinerated, as were tiny cycle repair shops, shoe shops and iconic Irani restaurants, run by families that had migrated from Persia in the early years of the twentieth century. The police looked on, impassive.

The police sympathy for Thackeray's party became even more obvious on the morning of 11 January, when the army stopped a car carrying Shiv Sena legislator Madhukar Sarpotdar and found two revolvers and two choppers inside. Sarpotdar was handed over to the police but let off, mystifyingly, for lack of evidence. Later that day, *Saamna* hit the streets with a new call. 'Enough is enough', it said. 'The fanatics have been taught a lesson. Now stop this violence.' That second round of barbarism had claimed 557 lives. Though Muslims formed only 15 per cent of Bombay's population, they constituted 63 per cent of the dead over the two months.

The government eventually appointed a high court

judge named B. N. Srikrishna to investigate the riots. But before that, at least three citizens' groups submitted their own reports, detailing the dynamics of the rioting in individual neighbourhoods, identifying mob leaders and making recommendations about administrative reform. One group would set up committees in the most troubled areas to give antagonistic neighbours a forum to start talking again. These mohalla committees would still be functioning twenty years later, keeping the peace at every tense moment.

On the afternoon of 12 March 1993, as I was returning from lunch, I saw smoke rising from the Stock Exchange Tower on Dalal Street. I hitched a ride on a passing fire engine and arrived to find utter devastation. A car bomb had gone off in the basement, killing dozens of people. Within minutes, I heard another roar in the distance. I began to run to the place it had originated, and fifteen minutes later, found myself outside the Air India building in Nariman Point. Listening to police radio in the car of an intelligence officer of my acquaintance, we learnt about bombs exploding down Bombay's spine: at the Zaveri Bazaar jewellery market, the passport office in Worli, at Plaza Cinema in Dadar, at a petrol pump next to the Shiv Sena headquarters, at SeaRock Hotel in Bandra. There would be ten in all, between 1.20 p.m. and 3.55 p.m. They would kill 257 Bombayites.

The authorities investigated the blasts and prosecuted the guilty with an efficiency that was remarkable, especially compared with their lethargy in punishing the perpetrators of the riots. Hundreds of people were rounded up. The wives and aged parents of some missing suspects were locked away in the cells of Mahim police station until their relatives turned themselves in. A special court was established to try the conspirators. By contrast, the riots commission, which only had the powers to identify culprits but not punish them, had a choppier journey. In 1996, after the judge had been at work for three years, the Shiv Sena disbanded the commission. It took a great deal of public pressure to have the commission reconstituted. When it finally delivered its report in 1998, naming senior politicians and thirty-one policemen for their complicity in the violence, the Srikrishna Commission's verdict was ignored.

The violence of those four tragic months seemed to seep into Bombay's very landscape, inuring the city to future injustices. At first, Bombay would turn a blind eye to obvious transgressions, pretending that compulsions of security demanded this. Soon, police hit squads would murder dozens of alleged criminals in extra-judicial killings that came to be known as 'encounters'. The official press releases would invariably claim that the police had been fired upon in the course of missions to arrest dangerous gangsters and had no option but to shoot back in self-defence. Coroners' reports would show that many of the alleged criminals had been shot in the back. Before long, the belief that the ends justified the means would render Bombay oblivious to illegalities of all sorts—traffic offences, tax evasion, and real estate fraud. Bombay has since developed an eisegetical relationship with the law, interpreting it as per individual convenience.

The bomb blasts would spawn another myth: that of the 'spirit of Bombay'. The city's alacrity in getting back to work the day after the attacks led to the suggestion that the metropolis was infinitely resilient, that it could pick itself up and march back into the trains after any tragedy, no matter how cataclysmic. The first time I remember hearing the phrase was on an episode of the news programme *The World This Week*. Shortly after the blasts, it ran a short segment titled 'A Tribute to the Spirit of Bombay'. It was deeply moving; friends told me that the programme made them weep. Since then, however, Bombay's indomitable will has been hailed by its politicians and socialites with such regularity, it has become obvious that they've used this resilience as an excuse to absolve themselves of the need to take the difficult decisions necessary to actually make the city more liveable. The incessant invocation of Bombay's spirit is just an attempt to ignore the numbing of another little bit of its soul.

TWO

In 1992, Mumbra, forty kilometres from downtown Bombay, was a semi-rural town with a single country liquor bar. The settlement was popular with rock-climbers for its Nursery Rocks, boulders that were technically difficult to scale but so low that you wouldn't get hurt if you fell (which I did with comical regularity). Among the town's largest businesses was sand dredging in the Thane Creek, on whose banks it is located. The 1991 Census put Mumbra's population at 44,217. Twenty years later, Mumbra had expanded into a mini city of an estimated 800,000 people—more than 90 per cent of them Muslim. In the aftermath of the riots, waves of Muslims began to seek out safer neighbourhoods and to create new havens. The largest of the Muslim islands to emerge was Mumbra.

Mohammed Ali, who has taught in an Urdu-medium municipal school in Mumbra's Kausa section for thirty-six years, deals with the consequences of this population explosion every day. When he started teaching in 1976, the school had 600 students. Today, it has 6,000, only 350 of them Hindu. Though the school works in two shifts, each of its sixty rooms packs in three divisions of students. 'They're crammed in like cattle,' Ali told me. Classes are held in storerooms; students sit on the floor and spill into the corridors.

Mumbra proved attractive for members of the riot-battered community because it had a long presence of Konkani Muslims who owned land there. Since Mumbra is in Thane district, it lacks the stricter regulatory environment of Bombay; building codes are observed mainly in the breach. Thousands of flats were constructed rapidly, many of them substandard. In April 2013, one such illegal building crumbled as residents were returning from work in the evening, leaving seventy-four dead. This was the most destructive house collapse ever to occur in Maharashtra.

Though the threat of physical violence has receded over the years, working-class Muslims continue to gravitate towards Mumbra to avoid the discrimination they routinely face in finding homes in many parts of Bombay. Prejudice against Muslims is so prevalent, even Shabana Azmi, the respected actress, has complained that she and her husband Javed Akhtar were unable buy a flat of their choice. Though moving to Mumbra helps Muslims sidestep this bias, other problems remain. For instance, power cuts that last up to six hours a day are routine here, even though Hindu-dominated Kalwa and Diva nearby face daily outages of only two hours. The flow of electricity determines the rhythms of life in Mohammed Ali's home. Baths can be taken only if there's power; without it, water can't be pumped from the underground storage tanks to the overhead cisterns. In the evening, his children try to finish their homework before twilight, to avoid draining the batteries their father has set up. With the power supply so erratic, his neighbours have great difficulty keeping up with the tortuous plots of the television serials they try to follow. Even getting a computer printout of a résumé to send out with a job application can mean waiting for hours.

Most of all, Mumbra residents say, they have no defence against their neighbourhood being stereotyped as a safe house for terrorists. Over the past decade, the police claim to have arrested several terrorists in the neighbourhood. The most notorious case involved a nineteen-year-old Mumbra college student named Ishrat Jahan Shamim Raza, who was killed by the Gujarat police in an encounter in 2004. They claimed she was on a mission to assassinate Gujarat's chief minister, Narendra Modi. However, a magistrate's report later said that senior police officers had staged the killing to win promotions.

While Mumbra is the largest Muslim enclave in the Bombay region, the demographics of other neighbourhoods have changed because so many others moved out. That was the case in Bandra Plot, in Jogeshwari, the site of some of the most bitter violence in '93. It is the neighbourhood that houses Radhabai Chawl, where six members of the Bane family were burnt to death. The squat, single-storey building in which they lived now houses a youth centre that conducts computer classes and helps members understand how to obtain ration cards, PAN cards and passports. On the face of it, the Aagaz Youth Development Centre would seem like a perfect symbol of reconciliation. But its administrator, twenty-nine-year-old Ismail Sharif, admitted that appearances are deceptive. During the riots, every one of the approximately twenty families who lived in the gully in which Radhabai Chawl is located was Hindu. Now, only two or three remain.

In Bandra Plot, as in Mumbra, residents claim that their neighbourhood has been stigmatized. They suggest that Jogeshwari East has been classified as a 'red zone' by banks, so applications bearing the 400 060 post code are routinely refused loans and credit cards. 'It's so bad, we can't even get post-paid mobile phone connections,' said Sharif.

The emergence of these enclaves has enlarged Bombay's vocabulary. Many Bombayites blithely refer to Jogeshwari as 'mini Pakistan', a term that is routinely applied to every Muslim-majority neighbourhood. The notion that all Muslims harbour sympathies for India's northwestern neighbour is so commonplace, in 2012, residents of one such locality in Nalasopara discovered that the bills issued by the state-owned electricity company listed their address as 'Mini Pakistan'. It stands to reason that the edges of the settlements are perceived as 'borders', both by residents and their Hindu neighbours. The simple act of traversing a street has been transmuted into an unreasonably risky undertaking.

Over time, prejudice against Muslims has become

so ingrained in Bombay life, the most vitriolic anti-Islamic sentiments can be expressed in polite drawing rooms without an eyebrow being raised. During a recent election, a mysterious organization called the Save Bandra Committee sent out fliers to Roman Catholic voters in my neighbourhood, where large numbers of Muslims have bought homes since the riots, claiming that Christians were being marginalized. It suggested that the influx had so altered the composition of the old Catholic strongholds of Ranwar and Pali, they would soon be given the Muslim names of Anwar and Ali. The handbill barely drew comment, let alone outrage.

P. K. Shajahan, an associate professor at the Tata Institute of Social Sciences, has spent several years trying to understand how the aftershocks of the riots were playing out in Mumbra, Jogeshwari and Dharavi—or, as he put it, how young Muslims are being affected by this 'socio-spatial relegation' to the margins. In all three neighbourhoods, he understandably found a deep sense of alienation. 'Space and identity have combined to become a deadly zone of exclusion,' he told me. 'They are disconnected from larger social processes—not for any fault of their own.'

Even as Bombay's Muslims are being pushed to the peripheries, other groups are voluntarily disconnecting themselves from people who aren't like them. The city's Jains, Marwaris and Gujaratis have bought up large tracts of Malabar Hill to establish building societies that only accept vegetarians as members. So repulsed are they at the thought of flesh that a restaurant that had the temerity to open on Malabar Hill a few years ago with meat dishes on the menu was battered out of business as its neighbours spat at clients and threw nails at them. (Evidently, the vegetarian belief in protecting all living things from harm didn't apply to humans.) Fear of losing the business of these well-heeled grass-eaters has prompted most upscale restaurants within a two- or three-kilometre radius of Malabar Hill to banish meat, fish and eggs from their tables. In the only Shiv Sena action that made me laugh, party members stormed several Malabar Hill vegetarian buildings in 2003 to brandish packets of Bombay duck, that abominably odorous fish, under the noses of residents. 'We have identified such buildings and will open non-vegetarian stalls next to them', the mob leader threatened, adding a rider that, regrettably, didn't seem to apply to his own associates: 'If they want to live in our city, these people will have to accept everyone'.

THREE

One evening in December 2012, less than a month after Bal Thackeray, the founder of the Shiv Sena, died at the age of eighty-six, I rode a construction elevator to the fortieth floor of an incomplete building right opposite the party headquarters in Dadar to listen to a jazz concert. When it is finished, Kohinoor Square is expected to rise 203 metres. Already, its glass facade is visible far across Bombay. The recital on the chic, distressed concrete slab by the pianist Louiz Banks was an excuse for the real estate company to invite Bombay high society to get a glimpse of the project that advertised itself as 'opulence personified'. Banks had composed a special tune for the occasion called *Raindrops on the Balcony*.

The twilit views were stunning. Bombay was aglitter with street lamps, car headlights, red warning lights atop buildings and cool-blue neon advertisements. On the western periphery of the makeshift concert hall, a pair of binoculars had been mounted on a stand to allow guests to look out at the Bandra-Worli Sea Link. As I peered through it, there was a burst of frenetic activity at the bottom of my field of vision. A group of men in nearby Shivaji Park, where Thackeray had been cremated weeks before, were gesticulating animatedly. Thackeray's followers had demanded that a memorial to their leader be constructed on the section of the park on which his pyre had stood. The state government had refused, so the Sainiks had thrown a cordon around the ashen site, just a block away from the beach their sympathizers had patrolled twenty years before to ward off the dreaded Iranian commandos.

Viewed from the heights of Kohinoor Square, as hostesses in black cocktail dresses conducted guests to their seats, the heat and dust of the political battle seemed very far away. That, of course, was exactly the illusion that the jazz concert was attempting to create. The company that is constructing Kohinoor Square is owned by the family of Manohar Joshi, one of Thackeray's most trusted lieutenants; until recently, his business partner was Bal Thackeray's nephew, Raj. They had bought the 4.8-acre plot in 2005 for Rs 421 crore. Four years later, Raj Thackeray—who had since formed his own political party, the Maharashtra Navnirman Sena—sold his stake for a reported profit of Rs 300 crore. Days before the jazz concert, the Sena's opponents had suggested that the memorial for Bal Thackeray should be built not in the public park but in the compound of Kohinoor Square, since it was owned by people who obviously held the Sena leader in high regard. The Joshis were trying their best to make the idea go away.

The controversy about the Thackeray memorial demonstrated how the political party that had risen to power championing the interests of the sons of the soil was now more concerned with profiting from the real

estate beneath their feet. It was the logical culmination
of an enterprise that started on the evening of 30
October 1966, when Thackeray addressed his first
public meeting. An invitation in Thackeray's magazine,
Marmik, requested readers to gather at Shivaji Park
if they were 'ready to bring about a Maharashtrian
resurgence'. When the cartoonist started the magazine
six years earlier, *Marmik* had been filled with social
and political cartoons. But since 1963, it had been
publishing the names of non-Maharashtrians who
held senior positions in the corporate sector. The lists
ran under the headline 'Read and Rise Up'. Marathi
speakers, Thackeray declared, were being marginalized
in the capital of their own state, especially in the business
world.

Unlike previous generations of Maharashtrian
reformers, who believed that social change should
start with self-improvement, Thackeray had an easier
solution: he blamed outsiders for Maharashtrians
failing to find jobs in the city's private sector. In May
1966, he formed a youth organization to combat
the perceived injustices to the Marathi manoos. He
called it the Shiv Sena—Shivaji's Army, invoking the
warrior king who had carved out an empire in the
region in the seventeenth century. In time, Bombay's
largest museum, one of its main train stations and
both its airport terminals, domestic and international,
would come to be named after Shivaji, resulting in
many confused passengers missing their flights, but

presumably reinforcing Maharashtrian pride.

Thackeray's Dussehra rally was to become an annual event and, at the half a dozen I attended over the years, it was clear that his early experience as a cartoonist had shaped his rhetorical style. With his horn-rimmed glasses and his skinny frame, he resembled a young Woody Allen, tossing out punch lines to devastating effect. Thackeray—who was routinely referred to in the press as the Sena 'supremo'—was never one to shy away from crudity. He devised obscene nicknames for his opponents and frequently reached for the pun. At his first meeting in 1966, for instance, he told the estimated 500,000 people in attendance that he intended to limit himself to social work because 'rajkaran [politics] is like gajkaran [the skin disease, ringworm]'. On their way home, some members of his audience attacked an Udupi restaurant—the generic name for eateries run by people hailing from the region of that name in Karnataka. South Indians would be the Sena's first targets, but as the decades passed, it would opportunistically set its sights on communists, Muslims and north Indians. Its xenophobia would find expression in the title of a promotional film produced by a senior party leader, which was later adopted as a rallying cry: 'Sundar Mumbai, Marathi Mumbai'—A Beautiful Bombay is a Marathi Bombay. By the 1990s, seeking to stretch his umbrella over even more potential voters, Thackeray appointed himself Hinduhridaya Samrat—Emperor of Hindu Hearts.

Early on, Thackeray urged Maharashtrian youth to demonstrate more enterprise. He suggested that they should set up stalls on the pavements to sell vada pao—batata vadas tucked into a loaf of bread. The very name of the snack was an acknowledgement of Bombay's multiculturalism: both batata and pao were Portuguese words that had found their way into Marathi. But in Thackeray's hands, vada pao became an excuse for Sena followers to usurp public space under the guise of restoring regional pride. Thackeray's enthusiasm for having a Marathi speaker in every job was so intense, he declared that he wanted to see the red-light district filled only with Maharashtrian prostitutes. From the Sena's foot soldiers selling snacks on the pavement to the Sena's generals starting construction companies was but a short leap.

Though Thackeray often expressed a visceral hatred of Pakistan, his politics were an uncanny reflection of dynamics across the border in Karachi. Both Bombay and Karachi are located in provinces that are deeply suspicious of the multi-ethnic enclaves on their coasts. But while the Sindhis have never quite managed to wrest control of Karachi from the Mohajir migrants who arrived there after Partition, Maharashtrians have had a significant presence in the Bombay municipality since Independence.

Maharashtrian anxiety about Bombay had been pronounced even before Thackeray arrived on the scene. It had been throbbing since 1953, when a commission was established to reorganize Indian states along linguistic lines. A group of industrialists lobbied for Bombay to be declared an autonomous city-state. In 1956, Prime Minister Jawaharlal Nehru announced that the vast territory known as Bombay State would be divided into the provinces of Maharashtra and Gujarat, while Bombay city would become a Union Territory, administered by the central government. Protests followed, leaving eighty people dead in police firing. Political parties, both Left and Right, formed a coalition called the Samyukta Maharashtra Samiti (the United Maharashtra Committee) to demand that Bombay become a part of their state. Their efforts worked. When Maharashtra was born on 1 May 1960, Bombay was its capital. With that, the city lost one of its greatest advantages: its unique configuration of interests and communities in which no group was completely dominant. Gujarati businessmen began to focus their attention northwards, and, as was to be expected, Marathi speakers came to dominate public life.

But as Bal Thackeray had realized, this did not immediately result in more jobs for Maharashtrians. Though Hindi speakers were more numerous in the city, south Indians became the Sena's first victims because they held many of the clerical jobs that Maharashtrians aspired to gain. The fear that Maharashtrians were being outnumbered in the state capital was unfounded. In 1961, shortly after *Marmik* was set up, Marathi speakers formed 43 per cent of Bombay's population, the largest linguistic group in the city. Just as shallow was Thackeray's suggestion that the Sena represented all Maharashtrians. The Sena was clearly antagonistic towards Marathi-speaking Dalits and Muslims from the Konkan and Marathwada. East Indians—who claimed to be Bombay aboriginals—were too numerically insignificant to matter.

If Thackeray thrived in those early years, it was because he had the indulgence of the Congress party. The Sena proved a useful counterbalance against the Left-wing parties that were popular in the central districts in which the textile mills were located. The Congress party had much to gain from undermining the communists and socialists because it had effected a legal legerdemain to keep a lock on the sole textile union that had the power to negotiate on behalf of mill workers. Thackeray was glad to play along. In September 1967, he wrote an editorial declaring that one of the Sena's primary objectives was the 'emasculation of the Communists'. Bombay's industrialists were also pleased to encourage the party of strike-breakers, even if they were never certain in which direction the loose cannons would fire. Executives of private-sector companies whose rolls did not reflect adequate numbers of Marathi-speakers were routinely assaulted, as were government officials who failed to fulfil the Sena's demands. Thackeray explained away the violence with another of his puns: sometimes thokshahi, the use of force, he said, was better than lokshahi, democracy.

Along with its strong-arm tactics, the Sena established itself as an arbiter of power at the neighbourhood level by helping constituents negotiate with officials to obtain municipal services and setting up ambulance corps at its numerous offices (which would soon be reconstructed with battlements to look like Shivaji's forts). Through the 1970s and '80s, the party began to win increasing numbers of seats in the municipal election.

Despite its growing popularity, though, the Sena proved unable to address the discontent of the city's 250,000 mill workers—the vast majority of whom were Maharashtrian—with the Congress-led union that represented them. Though many workers sympathized with the Sena's nativist rhetoric, they had little faith in the party's ability to negotiate effectively with the powerful mill owners. They believed that Thackeray's previous attempts to mediate with their employers had been high-handed and failed to keep their interests in mind. Others thought that Thackeray had discredited himself by supporting the Emergency called by the Congress only a few years before. So in October 1981, hundreds of textile workers marched sixteen kilometres from their mills in central Bombay to Ghatkopar, the home of Datta Samant, an independent labour organizer with a reputation for militancy. They demanded that he become their leader. Samant refused, so they sat outside all night until he caved in.

When employees of Bombay's forty-seven privately

owned mills and thirteen public sector mills launched a
strike in January 1982, there was euphoria in Girangaon,
the village of mills in which the majority of textile
workers and their families lived. The neighbourhood
had a social cohesion that gave mill workers a sense
of unity that was more intense than the ties between
employees in the city's other industries. Tens of
thousands of mill workers joined rallies to demand
higher wages and revised union rules. Trucks of grain
started to arrive from their home districts as farmers
demonstrated their support for the struggle.

The agitation dragged on for eighteen months. In
time, the loss of wages began to erode the workers'
resolve. Thousands went back to their villages. Others
were forced to pawn household objects or pull their
children out of school. Mill managements began to bus
scabs past the picket lines, aided by gangsters.

When the strike petered out, managements were
determined to ensure that workers in the country's
largest organized sector would never assert themselves
so decisively again. Several mills opened only partially,
while others stayed shut. Approximately 100,000
workers were not rehired and their dues were not
easily forthcoming. Curiously, at the end of the strike,
production had not fallen. Owners had simply moved
spinning and weaving operations to sweatshops in the
nearby towns of Bhiwandi and Malegaon.

The enormous pool of newly unemployed textile
labourers provided the Sena with fresh recruits. Its

neighbourhood networks offered the humiliated workers an alternative vision of community, one based not on class solidarity but defined by linguistic and religious values. When the riots broke out in 1992, men who had marched together exactly a decade before to demand economic justice turned ferociously against each other.

The momentum of the violence carried the Shiv Sena into power in Maharashtra in 1995, in partnership with its ideological sibling, the Bharatiya Janata Party. Manohar Joshi, who would go on to build Kohinoor Square, was appointed chief minister. Bal Thackeray, as always, believed that rajkaran was below him. But he reassured his supporters that he'd be making all the decisions. He laid out his techno-utopian vision of leadership in an editorial in *Saamna*: 'I have the *remote control* of politics and the *remote control* will continue to remain with me'.

Among the first signals Thackeray conveyed to the government was his decision to change the city's name from Bombay to Mumbai—though, as many noted, the Sena was merely restoring to the city its original identity. The name Mumbai, it's clear, honours the Koli goddess, Mumbadevi, a deity who, like many residents of her city, knows something about migration and compromise. Her shrine had originally stood next to the Phansi Talao, the gallows pond, near Bori Bunder. But in 1737, when the walls of the Fort were being constructed, Mumbadevi's temple moved northwards at the request of the authorities. Under most circumstances, the erasure of a colonial identity would have been welcomed by everyone. But coming as part of the Sena's campaign of hate, the rechristening of the city is still remembered for what it is—a refutation of Bombay's inclusive history. Disconcertingly, the Sena had seduced a globalized city to aspire to provincialism. Though the words Kolkata and Chennai roll easily off my tongue, Mumbai sticks in my craw. To me and most of my friends, the city will always be Bombay.

FOUR

As I potter around my section of Bandra, which has cottages from the 1940s and buildings from the early 1990s, I have a clear view into most compounds—and the people inside them of me. Most of the boundary walls have a concrete base as high as my knee, topped with grilles of metal or concrete that rise to my sternum. Friends playing with their children and older folk taking their exercise yell out greetings or flash a smile. Until a few years ago, groups of teenagers would perch on some walls to watch the world go by. These community-nurturing wall standards had been established in the 1930s, when building codes restricted boundary heights to five feet, the last one-third of which had to be latticework that permitted visibility.

But in 1991, as India began to restructure its economy to make it more transparent, a new set of building and land-use rules was instituted in Bombay that permitted the heights of compound walls to rise to 6.5 feet, going up to 7.4 feet in some circumstances. In contemporary Bombay, high walls are what distinguish older neighbourhoods from new ones, and recent complexes in long-settled neighbourhoods from apartment blocks constructed two or three decades ago.

The city's recent fondness for walls has diminished its pleasures in all sorts of ways. One of the minor joys of riding the Western Railway past Wankhede Stadium on match day was the opportunity to catch a glimpse of the pitch through gaps between the stands. In my time, I've had serendipitous visions of Vivian Richards taking guard before the wicket and Sachin Tendulkar dashing across the field. These sightings from the windows of trundling trains were necessarily fleeting, but they lightened a desultory day. Since the World Cup tournament of 2011, however, corrugated metal sheets have been propped up on the stadium's periphery—only at the two sections through which commuters could peer at the field. When I called the architect who designed the stadium to inquire why, he was rueful. 'Security concerns,' he explained.

But lengthening walls, it turned out, were only a minor effect of the Development Control Regulations of 1991. The rules were an eloquent articulation of the conviction that the invisible hand of the market would fix all Bombay's problems and were designed to transform the way the city lived and worked. In the months before the rules were announced, decision makers had begun to suggest that Bombay could be redeemed if it was repositioned as a global financial centre, processing the world's transactions in the hours that New York was going to sleep and Tokyo hadn't yet woken up. The DC rules were aimed at remaking Bombay to meet the requirements of the volatile FIRE sector that had come to dominate New York and London, home to the world's leading Finance, Insurance and Real Estate firms.

Working on the assumption that manufacturing was a futile activity in the world-class city that Bombay's elites aspired to build, the DC rules attempted to re-engineer the economy to foster the expansion of the service sector over traditional industries. The most dramatic provision of the rules permitted textile mills to sell the land on which they stood. This was a contentious stipulation. In 1991, despite the downsizing that followed the textile strike of 1982, the mills still employed 80,000 people. No one had devoted any thought to retraining them to find jobs in other sectors.

But even as the DC rules summarily dispensed with Bombay's textile workers, they offered the space-starved city of 9.9 million an unbelievable opportunity to reinvent itself. There was a rider to the clauses allowing mills to sell their land. Factories cashing in would have to surrender one-third of their plots for public housing and another third for open space and civic amenities. Since Girangaon's fifty-four mills stretched out over 600 acres in the heart of the island city, this was the chance for the congested city to breathe again and house its poor in dignity. The noted architect Charles Correa was appointed to draw up an integrated plan for the neighbourhood, knitting together the individual plots of mill land, most of which were larger than ten acres, by creating new thoroughfares and widening existing roads.

But as always, there was the Bombay loophole. Mills wouldn't have to surrender any land for housing and parks if they sold less than 15 per cent of their plots and used the proceeds to modernize their machinery. Soon, textile barons began to sell off slivers of their land, but then forgot to plough the funds back into their mills or pay their workers. Five years after the land sales had started, I volunteered with a human rights organization that was studying Girangaon's metamorphosis. For months, we listened to residents complain about how the impulse to turn Bombay into a shabby approximation of Singapore, the City of the Lion, was destroying the fabric of the place they'd known as Shrampur, the City of Work. To illustrate how his locality was changing, one former mill worker complained that chicken butchers were vanishing. It was proof, he said, that poultry-eating Maharashtrian and Muslim residents were being eased out of Girangaon and that vegetarian Gujarati and Jain traders were taking their place.

In 2001, without any public discussion, the rule relating to mill land sales was modified again, this time to absolve mill owners of any responsibility towards the city's future. The amended regulation clarified that the two-thirds rule did not apply to the entire plot on which their factories stood, but only to the open spaces between structures, such as the courtyards and passageways. The original formulation gave Bombay 400 acres of land on which to re-imagine itself. The revised version would free up only about fifty acres—and shatter any prospect of implementing a holistic plan for the neighbourhood. Citizens' organizations eventually caught on to the surreptitious amendment, but it was too late. Their challenge was dismissed by the Supreme Court in 2006. With that, the owners of Girangaon's mills began to develop their plots piecemeal.

By the new millennium, many of Girangaon's mills had become construction sites for glass-fronted office complexes, malls and vaastu-optimized gated communities like Island City Centre, projects that looked like they could have been located in Houston, Dubai or Kuala Lumpur. In their publicity material, they boasted that their grounds would have broad roads and spacious parks—facilities that all visitors to the area would have been able to enjoy if the mill owners had not blocked the integrated development plan.

Cannily, many of these complexes have managed to deprive Bombayites of even the minuscule amount of open space the mills were required to surrender. They've done this by locating the public parks deep within their compounds and allowing access to them for only a few hours each day. Few outsiders know of the existence of these green spaces and even if they do, they're often too intimidated by the security guards to actually use them. That's a criminal shame in a city that offers each resident about 1.1 square metres of open space—a figure that includes pavements and traffic islands. (Londoners have 31.6 square metres each to gambol about in.)

Such fragmentary development, with gleaming

private compounds in the midst of ill-serviced neighbourhoods, isn't unique to Girangaon: it has become Bombay's defining feature. Like so much else, this ad hoc urbanism is the result of processes triggered by the DC rules, which contained clauses ensuring that any attempt to implement rational urban plans in Bombay would thereafter be impossible. Until 1991, the size of a building depended on FSI, or Floor Space Index, a ratio that determined the height of a proposed structure in relation to the size of the plot on which it would stand. FSI paid heed to the holding capacity of a locality, taking into account the size of the water pipes and the drains, the width of the roads and other infrastructure. But the new rules allowed building rights to be traded like a commodity, turning FSI into Bombay's most valuable acronym. They opened the way for buildings to be constructed without considering the context of the neighbourhoods in which they were set. As a result, humungous towers have shot up in narrow lanes across the city, blocking air and light, causing traffic jams and water shortages around them.

119

Many loopholes were opened to allot construction companies extra building rights. Projects could be higher if developers promised to build parking spaces for public use, for instance, or if they rehoused residents of dilapidated old structures. They were allowed to build over portions of public parks in exchange for maintaining them. I was reminded how blurry the rules were recently as a rash of jewellery stores and offices erupted down Turner Road in my neighbourhood, which is zoned to be residential. Commercial complexes cannot be constructed on streets that are narrower than forty feet, so these buildings seemed, on the face of it, to be illegal. They weren't, of course. They'd been constructed under a clause that exempted information technology parks from the rule relating to road widths; once the permissions had been granted, no one had the time to check whether the buildings were actually being used by software geeks.

Real estate developers—many of whom had taken to describing themselves as 'infrastructure firms', as if this affords them a higher sense of purpose than mere land-sharking—are making too much money to even pretend to be bothered by the damage their projects are inflicting on the urban fabric. Anticipating these disasters should be the responsibility of the bureaucrats and politicians who are framing the rules. But they didn't seem to devote much thought to this either. Perhaps it's because, as a series of exposés have demonstrated, many of the administrators who are framing the regulations and the politicians who are approving them have stakes in real estate firms. If this seems to constitute a conflict of interest, no one is unduly bothered.

That is obvious from the publicity material for Manohar Joshi's Kohinoor Group, for instance, which is building Kohinoor Square on a plot once occupied by Kohinoor Mill. Its holdings include hotels, technical schools and wind-energy farms. One company brochure carries pictures of the former chief minister leading the ground-breaking ceremony for the thirty-eight-acre Kohinoor City development in Kurla and, a few pages later, addressing parliament. The document notes that Joshi had started life as an acting assistant temporary clerk in the municipal corporation, but his 'refusal to blink even while negotiating the uncharted paths translated into an immensely satisfying public life and a business empire'.

Even as builder-politicians enacted policies that created chaos in the streets, they were constructing high-value residential projects that promised to shield clients from that disarray—and from the people who have the misfortune of living in it. New apartment blocks in Bombay employ high walls, tall podiums and other architectural screens to protect residents from even visual engagement with people deemed undesirable. To ensure that they're impregnable, the complexes use an assortment of high-tech gadgetry. Island City Centre, for instance, will be fitted with a security command centre, CCTV for 24x7 surveillance and smart-card restricted access. It still isn't clear exactly why residents of these complexes have chosen to barricade themselves away. Bombay's rate of break-ins and street crime is inexplicably low, especially for a city of such stupefying disparities. In fact, the high walls may actually increase the prospect of crime by denying pedestrians the protective gaze of eyes on the street from the residents of the buildings around.

FIVE

When US President Barack Obama visited Bombay in November 2010, his mission was clear: he wanted to strengthen trade connections between the US and India. His speech to Indian government officials and businessmen against the backdrop of the Gateway of India made that evident. He said that the US saw India as a growing economic force and a strategic trade partner. He praised India's commercial capital for being a 'city of dreams' and then, bafflingly, singled out for special attention the residents of the 'winding alleys of Dharavi'.

Only a few years ago, the upper-crust guests in Obama's audience would have gasped at any reference by a foreign dignitary to the neighbourhood popularly (and mistakenly) referred to as Asia's largest slum. (In reality, Orangi in Karachi is even larger.) India's elite have always been prickly about Westerners drawing attention to their country's poverty, even though the World Bank estimates that about 80 per cent of the nation's population gets by on less than $2 a day. Instead, Obama's invocation of the 175-hectare slum drew hearty applause.

Of course, very few of the city's affluent set have actually walked through Dharavi or the other slums it has come to represent. If they did, they'd most likely be offended by the faecal odour that hangs over some parts of the neighbourhood, a consequence of the fact that 'open defecation', as bureaucrats know the practice, is widely prevalent there. Many of Dharavi's residents are forced to resort to this indignity because the neighbourhood has only one toilet stall for every 600 people.

But in addition to providing homes (with inadequate sanitation) for an estimated 600,000 people, Dharavi is filled with hundreds of workshops that turn out garments and biscuits, plastic bottle caps and leather purses. Dharavi is also an important hub in Bombay's recycling trade. Ragpickers from across the city converge on the slum every day to sell plastic bottles, strips of metal and rusty circuit boards to scrap traders there. These raw materials are melted down into ingots, to find life anew as plastic buckets or biscuit tins. In 2005, *The Economist* estimated the value of goods produced in Dharavi each year at $500 million.

It is this singular aspect of the neighbourhood that Obama alluded to in his speech, as he praised Dharavi's residents for their 'optimism and determination'. Obama's statement was probably intended to demonstrate both to his audience at home, reeling under a recession, and to Indian businessmen and policy makers, that Dharavi's diligent residents proved that the free market really did work, that anyone willing to strive hard had a shot at a better life. His Indian audience didn't take much convincing, even though evidence to the contrary stares them in the face every day. After two decades of structural adjustment, the proportion of Bombay residents living in shantytowns more than doubled from 23.5 per cent in 1991 to 48.8 per cent in 2011. It isn't as if they're occupying much more space, though. Slums cover just under 9 per cent of Bombay's land.

Unnervingly, the city's elite have come to see shantytowns as hubs of enterprise, as 'special economic zones' and 'city-systems' (though, of course, they don't want to be living right next to one of these 'user-generated cities'). Dharavi, perhaps because of the global popularity of the 2008 film *Slumdog Millionaire*, has come to embody the unimagined potential of Bombay's shantytowns. Never a week seems to go by without a newspaper, magazine or documentary exploring the wonders of Dharavi. Not so long ago, it became the focus of a self-help book titled *Poor Little Rich Slum*. In their introduction, the authors explain how they managed to look beyond 'the obvious—the garbage, the filth, the "sluminess" of the slum...[to see] beauty within the chaos.' They conclude: 'We can be happy, we can be hopeful, we can be enterprising—no matter where we are. They question is—are you? If Dharavi can, so can I'.

There could scarcely have been a more succinct declaration about why Dharavi is so useful for the elite of a city that houses just under half its residents in slums. Pretending that Dharavi is an oasis of opportunity absolves them of the guilt of ignoring the pitiful conditions in which their cooks, maids and drivers live. They have come to believe that life in the shanties and its sweatshops can't really be so bad if slum residents are able to be so productive.

The celebration of Dharavi's entrepreneurship is another piece of ideological legerdemain. The metamorphosis of Bombay's economy from one based on manufacturing to one in which the service sector is dominant has resulted in the large-scale casualization of employment. In 1951, the organized sector provided jobs for 72 per cent of the city's workers. This began to change dramatically with liberalization: the informal sector now accounts for at least two-thirds of the city's jobs. Hailing entrepreneurship as a supreme virtue makes individuals responsible for creating their own employment—and blames them for their misfortune. The celebration of slum entrepreneurship represents a comfortable compromise with existing structures of inequality.

The informalization in the sphere of work has imprinted itself on the city's landscape. Bombay is the embodiment in steel and curtain glass, blue tarpaulin and corrugated metal, of the inequalities of the new economic order. It's a heaving refutation of Trickle Down, proving malodorously that the creation of wealth for some doesn't directly result in the reduction of mass poverty.

Though the DC Rules of 1991 were aimed at making Bombay more attractive to foreign investors,

125

they didn't take the bait. Between 2007 and 2011, international capital created more jobs in Chennai, Bangalore and Pune than in Bombay. Indian businesses aren't expanding quite as quickly either. In the first quarter of 2013, more new jobs were to be found in Bangalore and Delhi. Even though one of Bombay's dearly held clichés maintains that no one willing to do an honest day's work will starve here, jobs that pay enough to support a family are increasingly difficult to find. As a result, one of five residents in India's most affluent city lives below the poverty line. That number soared by more than thirty-six times between 1999 and 2006. One study showed that 36 per cent of children in Bombay's slums are malnourished—significantly higher than the figure in most villages. Bombay's defenders often point out that all great cities are characterized by extremes of experience. But extremities are, by definition, the most intense ends of the spectrum. In India's commercial capital, a life on the margins is actually the predominant condition.

Since the 1990s, the situation has become even more precarious. Under the guise of a slum redevelopment scheme that was framed when the Shiv Sena was in power, an attempt is being made to evict shantytown residents from the slivers of real estate they occupy. Instead of building the sort of public housing projects that have proved effective in London, Hong Kong and Singapore, Bombay has decided that its housing crisis should be left to the whimsies of the private sector.

Construction firms have been offered land without cost and giddily high levels of extra FSI to build free homes for slum dwellers.

On the ground, the scheme isn't making much of a dent in solving the housing crisis. When the Slum Rehabilitation Act was passed in 1995, the Sena estimated that around 800,000 tenements would have to be built to house all the city's slum residents. More than a decade and a half later, the Comptroller and Auditor General reported that only 127,000 units had actually been constructed, even as the number of slum dwellers had grown enormously. In several cases, the intended beneficiaries have complained of fraud, that developers have been granted rights over entire plots on which slums occupy only a tiny portion, and that builders have inflated the number of slum dwellers on several plots in order to build more units than they're entitled to.

However, it would be unfair to dismiss the scheme as a complete failure: the incentives it offers developers for re-housing slum dwellers have facilitated the construction of some of the city's most expensive luxury blocks. These include the twin sixty-storey Imperial Towers in Tardeo, which have been built over a shantytown that spread across 13.5 acres. It has 228 apartments, each of which could sell for about $13.5 million. As per the provisions of the slum rehabilitation scheme, the 2,700 families who originally lived on the plot were given free homes of 225 square feet on the periphery of the development. Seven of their tenements could fit into the 2,000-square-foot swimming pool in the Imperial Towers penthouse. Even if the scheme hasn't been designed with the slum dwellers' interests in mind, it clearly makes sense for the developers, bureaucrats and politicians who allow it to continue. The slum rehabilitation programme, it's obvious, is an efficient mechanism for transferring into private hands the public land on which many slums stand. Along with the land acquisition strategies for Special Economic Zones and mining projects, the slum rehabilitation scheme is another example of what the geographer David Harvey describes as 'capital accumulation by dispossession'.

÷

In 2012, residents of several slum pockets indicated they that would no longer vacate their homes without a fight. Among the most energetic campaigns against the scheme was waged in Golibar, a 140-acre shantytown on the wrong side of the railway tracks from the eminently desirable neighbourhood of Khar. Golibar is the site of Bombay's largest slum rehabilitation project. Though many residents of the shantytown are attracted by the respectability of moving into a flat, they have alleged that the company undertaking the project, Shivalik Ventures, has not gathered the assent of 70 per cent of the neighbourhood's residents, as it is required to do by law. They claimed that the consent letters produced by the construction firm include the signatures of long-dead people and people who are illiterate. Golibar's residents have pursued their case through the courts and, when this proved too slow, they staged hunger strikes and street demonstrations. In several instances, they have formed human phalanxes to beat back the bulldozers and gone to jail to insist that they get a fair deal.

Their struggles are a startling echo of protests a century ago against a redevelopment project initiated in the late 1890s in the wake of the plague epidemic that left tens of thousands dead. The Bombay Improvement Trust of 1898 was ostensibly established to heal the diseased city by 'opening out crowded localities', 'constructing sanitary dwellings for the poor' and building wide streets. There was a good economic reason to do this. The epidemic had caused the city's population to drop by 6 per cent in the decade up to 1901, leaving the mills struggling to find workers. In an attempt to make the BIT more efficient, the organization was allowed to function independently of the oversight of the elected representatives of the municipal corporation. This, in effect, permitted the bureaucrats of the BIT to make autocratic decisions without the anxiety of being questioned about them. It also established a precedent for contemporary Bombay, in which more than a dozen agencies execute infrastructural projects without any central plan.

The BIT set about demolishing tenements so that they could be replaced by chawls for mill workers, and

129

began to construct such arteries as Sydenham Road (later renamed Mohammed Ali Road) and Princess Street. It didn't take long for the Trust to run into noisy opposition. Landowners, as was to be expected, protested that they had been inadequately compensated, but the residents of shantytowns were not happy either. They were not given alternative accommodation when their homes were torn down and when the new chawls came up, the rents proved unaffordable. Then, as now, the dispossessed slipped back into slums on the edges of the areas that were being improved, exacerbating the problem the BIT had set out to solve. Proof of the failure of the 'pseudo-sanitarians', as the Trust's supporters had been labelled by critics, came in 1919, when the government dissolved the organization. Though it had been at work for twenty-one years, 74 per cent of Bombay's residents still lived in one-room tenements.

A century after the BIT, Bombay's attempts to sanitize itself and transform itself into a world-class city continue to take heavy casualties. In addition to the residents being evicted for slum rehabilitation projects, thousands of others have been relocated because they were in the path of road and rail initiatives. About 60,000 of these 'Project-Affected Persons', as they're officially classified, have been shifted into about a hundred buildings in the northeastern area of Mankhurd. The buildings, seven to fourteen stories high, stand in the municipal ward with Bombay's worst human development indicators: average life expectancy is thirty-nine (compared to a citywide average of fifty-two); and the ward's population density is 66,881 per square kilometre (compared to 20,898 elsewhere).

Even though they have received their homes for free, many residents of the Mankhurd projects are not exactly overjoyed. Their 225-square-foot flats are too small for multigenerational families, they say, and the lifts frequently break down, inconveniencing old people and children on higher floors. The buildings are poorly ventilated and some stand ten feet or so away from each other. But mainly, as a construction labourer named Shiv Kumar complained to me, 'Mankhurd is too far from most sources of work.' Many of the area's daily wage earners and domestic workers say that their earnings are too low to allow them to commute to jobs in other places. The fatal flaw in the SRA and the BIT was identified by the Scottish urban planner Patrick Geddes in the 1920s, but has never been resolved. 'Bombay', said Geddes when he visited the tenements of the Bombay Improvement Trust, 'is not housing its workers—it's warehousing them'.

SIX

Almost since the city's inception in the seventeenth century, Bombay's infrastructure has fallen short of residents' requirements. Bombayites have always complained that the city was too crowded, dirty and noisy to be fit for human habitation. On my bookshelf, I have a whole section of pamphlets and papers warning of imminent collapse. The titles include *Revisioning Mumbai: Conceiving a Manifesto for Sustainable Development* (published in 2010), *Bombay by 2000 AD* (published in 1986) and *Bombay: Today and Tomorrow* (published in 1930).

Over the year in which I was researching this book, two national newsmagazines carried cover stories agreeing with these ominous predictions. 'Mumbai on the Brink: Twenty years after the last conflagration, India's city of hope is riven again by fear and communal tension', said *India Today*'s headline. Asked *Outlook,* 'Who Killed My Mumbai?: How did a City of Dreams, which gave life and hope to millions across the country, come to this sorry state?' It's a sentiment that *The Illustrated Weekly of India* had expressed on its cover four decades earlier, in September, 1974. 'Urban CHAOS', it screamed. 'Save Bombay—Now!'

Alongside its enduring passion for staring doom in the face, Bombay has demonstrated an unquenchable enthusiasm for organizing exhibitions and lectures about potential solutions for the city's problems (which are always referred to as 'challenges'). Though Bombay has been in a perpetual state of crisis, it has never stopped believing that its predicament could not be overcome by a good chinwag. The earliest symposium on the fate of the city was conducted by Patrick Geddes, who was appointed Bombay University's first professor of sociology and civics in 1919. He had made his reputation as a town planner with a City and Town Planning exhibition, which used maps and cardboard models to explain his humanist ideas to audiences in several places in the UK and Europe.

When he arrived in India, he discovered that the subcontinent's town planners, instead of trying to create cities that fostered community, were acting either like sanitation engineers or architects of an imperial fantasy. Geddes, on his part, was a proponent of participatory planning and of conservative surgery; rather than large-scale razing, he advocated selective clearances to open out cramped neighbourhoods. The bearded Scotsman laid out his exhibition at the Institute of Science in Colaba and accompanied it with a series of lectures. 'Town planning is not mere place planning or even work planning', Geddes said. 'If it is to be successful, it must be folk planning.'

Over the past few years, seminars and exhibitions about Bombay's future have seemed to open at the rate of one a week. Some of these events are organized

133

by citizens' groups and local research organizations attempting to stir the authorities into action. But many are international initiatives that bring to Bombay members of a new species known as 'urbanists'. (To my horror, I have on occasion been accused of being one myself.) Urbanists are the product of the recent academic obsession with cities, prompted by the forecast that 70 per cent of the world's population will live in cities by 2050. Academics have been especially fascinated by megacities like Bombay because seven of every ten people on the planet are expected to live in conurbations with more than ten million people by the middle of the century.

Urbanization, it's apparent, has the potential to transform lives. When people settle in cities, it's easier to provide access to education and medical aid, electricity and clean water. In addition, as much of the contemporary academic literature emphasizes, cities are powerful economic engines, generating jobs and potentially raising the standard of living of inhabitants. But the biggest advantages of urbanization are social. Cities can tear down traditional barriers and bring diverse people into contact, encouraging them to see the world in new ways. However, as Bombay residents well know, life in a megacity can also be hellish, especially for poor migrants. Even as the proponents of economic restructuring insist that India has no option but to jettison its Gandhian celebration of village life and embrace the 'growth potential' of urbanization, they're alarmed when the products of rural distress actually land up in the city and, having no option, move into slums. These competing scenarios are what draw urbanists from around the world to Bombay. They want to study what makes the city tick, but mostly, they come to learn from its mistakes.

Dharavi is, of course, a compulsory stop on every urbanist's itinerary. However, more discerning scholars also travel across the harbour, to a dormitory town that is a monument to Bombay's boundless capacity for messing up a potentially good thing. When the city of New Bombay was notified in 1970, its older namesake was struggling to deal with the task of housing 7.7 million residents. To ease the pressures, Bal Thackeray and his followers, most of whose parents had been migrants, suggested that entry to Bombay be regulated by permit. An idealistic group of urban planners proposed another solution: creating a twin city that would act as a counter-magnet for the hordes the Sena claimed were flooding into Bombay every day. As was often the case, the Sena had its facts wrong. Since 1961, natural increase—Bombay residents having children—had added more people to the city than migration. Nonetheless, everyone agreed that Bombay seemed stretched to capacity.

New Bombay was to be laid out on 55,000 acres to the east, across the bay. This would decisively break the linear flow of commuters from distant northern areas to the business district on the southern tip of the peninsula. Residents of New Bombay, it was hoped, would find jobs in the port of Nhava Sheva that was to be constructed nearby, as also in companies from the old city that would relocate there. Crucially, the plan envisaged that the state government would move its offices to the twin city, as also the state legislature.

The city across the water was to be defined by its public transport system. Housing clusters were to be located within a five-minute walk of transportation nodes, while cycling tracks would run everywhere. Poorer residents could buy serviced plots on which they could build rudimentary shelters, and expand them as their resources allowed. 'The effort has been to avoid the spectacular, to provide minimally for the affluent few and to promote the convenience of the greatest number', the plan said. 'New Bombay, then, will not be another Grand City; it will be a city where the common man would like to live.'

That definitely wasn't the sense I got one recent winter afternoon when I visited the Navi Mumbai Property Fair 2013. In an air-conditioned tent the size of an aircraft hangar, about a hundred real estate developers held out their enticements. As a Ukrainian accordion player in a black velvet jacket squeezed out jolly folk tunes, I wandered around picking up brochures for expensive apartment blocks in the new New Bombay, which was being built in Ulwe and Ghansoli, Vichumbe and Kamothe. There were so many developments to choose from: Shah Alpine in Kharghar and The Pacific near Shilp Chowk; Tulsi Heights in Kalamboli and Progressive's Highness off Palm Beach Road. Many of the glossy booklets claimed that their projects were really not that far from downtown Bombay, acknowledging that the twin city was just another bedroom destination. The brochures also made it clear that the complexes were for the affluent. One leaflet for a nineteen-storeyed building described the altitudinous project as 'the perfect complement to the heights' its well-off residents had reached. Another promised 'lavish work styles and elite lifestyles'. Despite the egalitarian objectives on which it was founded, New Bombay had evidently moved on.

Looking back, it seems clear that New Bombay had been set up to fail. Even though the Maharashtra government had emphatically declared its intention to decongest Bombay, it decided in the mid-1960s to revive the Back Bay Reclamation Scheme that had been abandoned after the scandal of the 1920s. The Congress government said that 80 per cent of the planned 550-acre district would be used for housing, and only 20 per cent for commercial buildings. The new neighbourhood, known as Nariman Point after the belligerent Congressman who halted the last attempt to reclaim the bay, would be dominated by a sixty-seven-acre central park. By 1975, only seventy-nine acres of land had been reclaimed and the project was proving just as contentious as its predecessor. Some plots—still underwater—had been sold at between fifty-six paise and sixty-four paise a square foot, far below prevailing market rates. Mysteriously, colour codes were changed on the development plans so that the vast majority of the land came to be allocated to office buildings. Nariman Point would become Bombay's first high-rise office district, drawing in more than 220,000 workers each day. Bombay's debilitating north-south axis had only been reinforced.

It wasn't just the eruption of Nariman Point that prevented New Bombay from acquiring a life of its own. The state government threw a spanner in the works by failing to relocate. In 1981, it cemented its decision to stay put in the old city by inaugurating a new legislative assembly building in the heart of Nariman Point. In interviews since then, New Bombay's designers have admitted that they should have expended greater energy on garnering political support for their city across the bay. But perhaps the failure of New Bombay is a reminder that, no matter how sophisticated the plans, it's almost impossible to will into being a vibrant city in a year or two. Cities are the accretion of generations of debates about fish manure and street alignments, a layering of memories of eccentric music concerts and potty-mouthed demagogues. Even though the old metropolis of Bombay was bursting at the seams, it still offered residents something ineffable that inhibited them from moving across the water. Charles Correa, one of the planners of the new metropolis, summed up this dilemma elegantly when he noted that Bombay is a great city and a terrible place. No matter how burdensome life in Bombay seems to become, it's almost impossible to leave.

SEVEN

As motorists zip off the Bandra-Worli Sea Link, they are greeted by a signboard announcing, 'South Mumbai'. The arrow on it actually points north. Vehicles must drive the wrong way for about 150 metres before taking a U-turn at a traffic circle that sends them back in the direction they actually need to be heading. Since it was opened in 2009, Bombay residents of a certain class and disposition have come to celebrate the bridge as a symbol of the city's possibilities. As it turns out, the sea link is a more literal metaphor for Bombay than they realize.

The bridge cost five times more than estimated and took ten years to build—twice as long as anticipated. But it isn't just the awkward engineering, inordinate delays and financial inefficiency that make this bridge a reliable indicator of the foolhardy path Bombay has chosen. While 7.2 million people shove their way into the overburdened train system each day, the sea link is used by only 40,000 vehicles—a number that has been falling since the bridge was opened. Privileging infrastructure for private vehicles over public transport is flawed urban policy and a mockery of democracy.

At the time of the riots, Bombay had only two flyovers. Today, it has approximately fifty-five, with more under construction. Over that period, only a handful of public transport projects were completed, notably the extension, in stages, of the railway line to New Bombay. Not surprisingly, the number of private vehicles has more than doubled since 1991, from 9.4 lakh to 18.7 lakh. Traffic moves at an average of ten kilometres per hour during peak hour—less than half the speed clocked by winners of the city's annual marathon. Despite this, people who support the idea of permits for migrants are aghast at the suggestion of a congestion charge for vehicles.

To watch Bombay traffic creeping ahead is to see the ferocious sense of entitlement of India's moneyed classes in motion. Bombay traffic refuses to give way to ambulances, and honks furiously at old people and schoolchildren trying to cross the street. It never stops at zebra crossings, frequently jumps red lights and routinely comes down the wrong way on no-entry streets. Because 60 per cent of cars are driven by chauffeurs, more than in most other parts of the world, car owners have the fig leaf of pretending that they aren't responsible for transgressions they actually encourage.

At first glance, the investment in road links in South Bombay flies in the face of the findings of the 2011 census: the population of the island city actually fell by 7.6 per cent over the previous decade, while the rest of Bombay grew at merely 8 per cent—the slowest rate since the 1920s. The new high-rise towers of South Bombay hold fewer people than the smaller structures they are replacing. Besides, with jobs and accommodation so scarce, Bombay isn't attractive to migrants any longer. But while the density of the island city has reduced, the intensity has been stepped up. When the economy was dominated by manufacturing, the urban planner Rupali Gupte has observed, most Bombay workers spent their entire day in a single factory or office. Now, with most people working in the service sector or being self-employed, there are jobs to be done in several places across the city every day. Though there are fewer residents in some parts of Bombay, they're making more trips, most often by road.

Queries related to roads formed the largest number of questions Bombay's elected municipal representatives posed to bureaucrats in 2012. Or, to be precise, their queries related to how they could rename Bombay's streets, presumably to humour their patrons. While the city fathers were concerned about the nomenclature of the streets, I'm in a perpetual fury about the pavements—where they actually exist. In recent years, pavements in my neighbourhood have been narrowed to give cars more space. Despite this, it isn't uncommon to find vehicles parked on the size zero sidewalks. My progress is also impeded by flowerpots, telephone junction boxes, open manholes, advertising hoardings disguised as bus shelters, car ramps to buildings rising a foot above the sidewalk, milk booths, STD shops and assorted hawkers. Pedestrians accounted for 57 per cent of the traffic fatalities in Bombay in the four years up to 2012 and, as someone who is given to volcanic displays of pedestrian rage at errant motorists, I fully expect to be counted among that number soon.

It wasn't like that in the movies. For a century, much of what India has known about Bombay has been from films—and that city of the imagination was a city of the streets. By the 1950s, the city that had followed Gandhi's call so enthusiastically had turned itself into the showpiece of Nehru's India, a melding of cultures and a mixing of economies, where, for a brief moment, it seemed like the private and the public would find a happy equilibrium. A thousand screen migrants caught their breaths as they exited into Bombay through the neo-Gothic gates of Victoria Terminus station (not yet renamed for the Maratha king), conducted melody-filled romances on Marine Drive (which had been completed in 1940 after reclamation off the Kennedy Sea Face) and marvelled at the mighty buildings as they trundled through Bombay in a kali-peeli taxi (which actually charged you the rate on the meter). Raj Kapoor's earnest tramp of the 1950s, Amitabh Bachchan's angry young man of the 1970s and the louche taporis who followed him in the early 1980s were all creatures of the Bombay street, flaneurs who spoke mishmash Hug-me like it was their native tongue.

For the last two decades, however, the Bombay film, like the upper middle classes it now counts as its primary audience, has retreated indoors—or fled to New Jersey. Bombay has become too ugly to serve as

143

the cradle for a fantasy and besides, shooting on the streets is impossible, what with vast crowds pressing in on every shot and corrupt policemen threatening to halt the action unless they're paid off, even though all permissions are in order. Even Bollywood, it seems, has abandoned its Bombay dream.

EIGHT

In 1971, my grandfather Ammon Rodrigues wrote a letter to Maharashtra's minister for urban development, P. G. Kher, requesting a resolution to a problem that had been irking him since 1959. With the notification of the Town Planning Scheme, Bandra No III that year, his 1,715-square-yard plot of farmland had been earmarked for a municipal maternity hospital. In exchange for his ancestral farm, the authorities were offering him a piece of land that was only half the size and which had several hutments on it. The authorities offered to compensate him for the discrepancy in the size of the plots at the rate of Rs 16 per square yard, which didn't seem fair.

Grandpa contended that the maternity home was entirely unnecessary since there were already several similar hospitals in the area, including one run by the municipality just a kilometre away. If they were set on building yet another hospital for new mothers, however, Grandpa suggested that the authorities should locate it on a portion of the plot opposite his that had been reserved for a recreation ground, to be known as the Khar Gymkhana. After all, it had 'been acquired at the expense of all landholders in the Scheme...and would not penalise only one individual plot holder like me', he noted.

It was a variation of the plea he'd been making for more than a decade to officials in the municipality and state government, none of whom seemed inclined to address his concerns. A few months ago, I picked through the eleven kilogram sack of letters and court petitions Grandpa had accumulated in his long years of trying to get a just deal. It presented a fascinating picture of how the farmlands of Bandra came to be absorbed into the big city.

Grandpa Ammon was ten years old when the plague carried away his father, Francis Xavier Rodrigues. His mother Asumpta, who spoke Marathi and Portuguese, struggled to bring up her son and two daughters. The epidemic took several years to ebb, so the family occasionally slept in the fields to avoid infection in the closed confines of Pali Village. The disease killed 608 people on average in each of the nine years from 1909. Reminders of those fearful times still mark the streets of Bandra in the form of Plague Crosses, erected by the faithful to seek protection from the disease or by grateful survivors. Grandpa was the first member of his family to go to school, taking the train into town to be instructed by bearded Jesuits at St Xavier's in Dhobi Talao. After he matriculated in 1916, he sought employment in a Greek trading firm. Summoned for an interview, he realized that he didn't own any long trousers, and had to borrow a pair from a more affluent cousin.

But the tribulations didn't dull Grandpa's sense of

wonder at the city's progress. Shortly after the new
Bassein Creek Bridge was completed at the end of
1925, he walked across its 1.8-kilometre span so he
could inspect the longest structure on the suburban
railways system at close quarters. One hot October
afternoon in 1932, he took a shorter stroll to Juhu
to see J. R. D. Tata land his Puss Moth at the Juhu
aerodrome with India's first cargo of air mail. The next
few years would bring water closets and septic tanks
to most Bandra homes, doing away with the odious
reliance on scavengers to carry away the night soil on
bullock carts. Electricity would illuminate homes, but
not the streets—gas lamps, lit by men carrying long poles
tipped by flames, would remain part of my parents'
memories of a 1950s Bandra childhood.

Bandra's tryst with urbanization had been
intensifying since 1867, when the sole daily train
service between Virar and Grant Road began to halt
there. This encouraged Parsis, Muslims and British
people from Bombay to build weekend retreats in the
neighbourhood. When the plague ravaged Bombay
in 1897, many people moved permanently because
Bandra's open spaces seemed safer than the congested
city. In 1911, the year Francis Xavier Rodrigues died,
Bandra's population stood at 22,800. By 1927, it had
added 6,000 more residents and, of course, it all seemed
like a terrible mess. 'On these verdure-clad slopes, the
palm-fringed shores and wide rice fields have risen
palaces and mansions, and yet Bandra seems to have

outgrown', grumbled Braz Fernandes, a relative on my father's side, in his book, *Bandra: Its Religious and Secular History*, published that year. 'The housing famine is acute.'

Still, even Fernandes was willing to concede that a few good things had come out of it. The passage of time had turned Bandra into that magical Bombay thing—'a cosmopolitan place', he admitted. Besides, 'under the magic wand of the Land Development Department, new roads and well-laid villages are springing up in rapid succession'. The idea of a town planning scheme for Bandra had been proposed in 1912 by a civil servant named E. G. Turner. At a meeting of architects, Turner noted that though the population of Bandra was expanding, the irregular shape of the farmlands and orchards made it difficult to find suitable plots on which to build homes. A town planning scheme, he said, would create evenly aligned roads and would allow for the creation of 'cheap water supply and other amenities'. If every plot holder surrendered 10 per cent of his land for amenities, real estate values would rise and benefit everyone, he said. But there was a price to be paid. 'In this rush of town planning', Fernandes wrote, 'most of the original small holders have been wiped out of the Collector's Records'.

Despite the belief that colonial administrators were nimbler than the Indian bureaucrats who inherited the steel frame, the planning scheme for Grandpa Ammon's neighbourhood was conceptualized in 1917, sanctioned

148

to take effect in 1940 but only published in 1955. By then, my grandfather had become an accountant in a trading firm called Rallis, so he'd handed over his plot to a cultivator, who occasionally dropped by with gifts of pumpkins and beans. Even though Grandpa, like other Bandra residents, said that he was 'going to Town' when he headed south to work each morning, Bandra's villages had officially become part of the city in 1950, when the suburb had been absorbed into the Greater Bombay Municipal Corporation. In 1957, the map was redrawn yet again to take the city's boundaries up to Borivali on the Western line and Mankhurd on the Central line.

The prospect of losing his most valuable asset drove Grandpa to explore every avenue he thought would bring relief and the creation of the new administrative district gave him even more officials to write to. In his files are scores of letters to successive municipal commissioners, urban development secretaries, district collectors and deputy collectors, ward officers and their assistants. In 1976, proving that one arm of the government really didn't know about what other departments were doing, Grandpa's agricultural plot got taken over a second time, this time under the Urban Land Ceiling Act. He finally filed suit against the acquisition and though the court eventually ruled that the authorities should give him an alternative plot, without any settlers on it, that piece of land never materialized. In 1983, as Grandpa was sick with cancer, he decided it wasn't worth battling

149

the bureaucrats any longer. He gave up his interest in his family farm.

The government, however, never seemed to find the funds to build that maternity hospital, so the cultivator continued to till the plot well into the early years of the twenty-first century. Until recently, I'd lead bemused friends past the vegetable patch amidst the forest of concrete. The expeditions always made me smile: here, after all, was literal evidence of my family's long roots in Bombay.

As I went by one day in 2010, I noticed that the cultivator was gone and that a trench was being excavated. Over the next few months, it became clear that they weren't building a hospital. Now, early in 2013, the finishing touches are being put on a sixteen-storey building. There's a slick advertisement for it on YouTube. 'A man's home is his castle', says the commentary. 'But here, in the city of dreams, to have a castle is a luxury reserved for the select few.' That fortunate minority, the promo said, would include clients discerning enough to shell out the money to live in Orchid Breeze—'a modern haven of luxury, style, comfort and convenience, all rolled into one'. Each apartment will cover the entire floor.

The project is being executed by a firm called DB Realty, one of whose promoters, Shahid Balwa, was arrested in 2011 for allegedly bribing the minister of telecommunications to obtain licences to run a cell phone company. To the side of Orchid Breeze, 25 per cent of the original plot has been sliced off for the proposed maternity hospital. A large tree stands in the middle of the driveway at the entrance, so it isn't clear how patients will enter when the facility begins to function. I've tried to peek into Orchid Breeze several times, but the walls are simply too high.

NINE

When the sky turned black that July afternoon in 2005, office workers across Bombay decided it would make sense to head out a little early and make for the safety of their homes. The rain was beating down rather heavily and, if it kept up, we all knew that the trains would pack up soon. Several members of the clerical staff of the magazine at which I worked made for the station but I had to stay put: there was, as always, a deadline to be met.

Over the next twenty-four hours, 37.2 inches would pour down on the city—75 per cent of the deluge in a five-hour period from 2.30 p.m. As the water rose to first-floor level in some places, more than 1.5 lakh people were stranded on railway platforms. With the roads turning into rivers, some people couldn't get out of their cars and drowned at the wheel. Others were stuck on the upper decks of buses. Hillsides caved in, houses collapsed, electricity poles came crashing down. The rains left 447 people dead—they were drowned, electrocuted or crushed to death by falling objects. The water gushed into tens of thousands of homes in low-lying areas and neighbourhoods with choked drains, destroying furniture, family keepsakes and lifetimes of hard work. The city that had been reclaimed from the ocean seemed briefly to return to it. As the waters receded, they brought into focus new islands—islands of the mind.

The 26 July rains had made apparent decades of wilful damage wrought on Bombay. Politicians and bureaucrats, in their eagerness to benefit builders, had disregarded all notions of sustainable development. Towers had been sanctioned without considering whether the water, sewage and storm water drainage lines in the area could support them. The destruction of mangrove swamps had reduced the area available for the rain water to drain. The worst flooding had occurred in the northwestern areas along the course of the Mithi river, which swelled dramatically and spilled its banks. That shouldn't have surprised anyone. Over a decade, the river's course had been diverted ninety degrees by the extension of a runway at the airport, its width narrowed by the Bandra Kurla Complex, and its mouth pinched by the Bandra Worli Sea Link. Middle-class Bombay, however, bandied about another explanation. Many obdurately believed that the Mithi's capacity had been reduced because slums such as Bharat Nagar had sprouted on its banks.

Faced with a catastrophe of this magnitude, most other cities would have swarmed into the street to demand immediate solutions from its politicians and administrators. Bombay contented itself with passing around SMS messages that thundered about the government's misdeeds. This was slacktivism at its best—and yet another sign of middle-class Bombay's inability to understand the source of the city's problems. Shortly after, the state government announced plans to allow construction on 5,500 acres of salt pan land, tidal tracts essential for monsoon water to drain, but no one seemed bothered enough to even text their ire.

Three years later, text messages were still the weapon of choice when Pakistani terrorists attacked CST station and prominent city hotels. 'Yes, we need to be scared about the people who came in on the boat but we need to be even more worried about the people who came in on our votes', claimed one especially motile message, highlighting anger at the failure of elected officials to provide clear direction during the sixty-hour crisis in 2008.

This time, middle-class Bombay actually found the energy to organize a public display of its anger. On 3 December 2008, an estimated 20,000 people made their way to the Gateway of India and promised not to rest until the administration completely overhauled the security system. Some banners at the rally urged residents to stop paying their taxes to protest against the government's failure to protect the city. Others encouraged citizens to refrain from voting during the next elections.

Then, just as quickly, the rage burnt itself out. At the Lok Sabha elections a few months later, they made good on their promise not to vote: only 43.3 per cent of eligible voters in South Bombay turned out to cast their ballots, even fewer than the 44.2 per cent who participated in the previous election in 2004. But it would probably be giving them too much credit to imagine that they'd boycotted the elections. They were simply too apathetic to stir themselves to vote.

Two decades after public services and spaces began to be privatized, Bombay's middle classes had become so enamoured of the pay-as-you-go approach, they'd come to view democracy as a consumer scheme. They were so eager to demand their rights, they'd completely forgotten about their fundamental duties. They were unable to understand that transforming politics would take much more than withholding their votes and their tax money: it would take zealously engaging with the system—and their poorer neighbours. But that is becoming increasingly difficult, as middle-class Bombay shops in access-restricted malls, exercises in parks operated by private developers, trades public transport for air-conditioned cars and aspires to live in gated communities.

The re-islanding of Mumbai does not bode well for its future. A city can flourish only if it has common ground to make common cause.

ACKNOWLEDGEMENTS

For commissioning articles that sprouted into sections of this book: Kaiwan Mehta at *Domus*, Niloufer Venkatraman at *National Geographic Traveller India* and Priya Ramani at *Mint-Lounge*.

For concepts, conversations and contacts: Amita Bhide, Anita Patil-Deshmukh, Ashok Datar, Charles Correa, Darryl D'Monte, Faiz Ullah, Faiza Khan, Girish Shahane, Gyan Prakash, H. M. Naqvi, Javed Iqbal, Jerry Pinto, Kaiwan Mehta, Kalpana Sharma, Kamu Iyer, Kiran Nagarkar, Matias Echanove, Murali Ranganathan, Mustansir Dalvi, Neera Adarkar, Pankhaj Joshi, Prasad Shetty, Prashant Kidambi, Rahul Srivastava, Ram Guha, Rishi Aggarwal, Rohan Shivkumar, Rupali Gupte, P. K. Das, Samir D'Monte, Sheela Patel, Simpreet Singh, Suketu Mehta, Teesta Setalvad, Vinod Shetty, Vidyadhar Date.

For helping me write the world beyond journalism: Michael McQuarrie, Harel Shapria, Cassim Shepard, Saskia Sassen, Richard Sennett, Craig Calhoun, Gerald Frug and the rest of the Poesis gang.

For finding elusive documents: Joan Dias, Gyan Prakash, Akshay Deshmane.

For reading the manuscript and pointing out many idiocies: Ranjit Hoskote and Nandini Ramnath. For giving my purple constructions and fanciful contentions the whipping they deserved: Katherine Boo.

For tramping around the city with me: Sidharth Bhatia, Vikram Doctor.

For enduring numerous rants about how it's all going to the dogs: Nandini Ramnath.

For parental indulgence: Lorna and Ernest Fernandes.

ONE

3   'pollution, crowds and noise': Advertisement for Sumit Greendale, *Mid-Day*, Hot Property, 2 November 2012.

3   'The urban landscape': Advertisement for Island City Center, *The Times of India*, 7 November 2012.

3   'reside at newer': Advertisement for Vasant Oasis, *Daily News and Analysis*, 22 December 2012.

3   'where a refreshing': Advertisement for Rodas Enclave, *The Times of India*, The Address, 23 November 2012.

3   'next-generation eco-friendly': Advertisement for Marathon NexZone, *The Times of India*, Times Property, 24 November 2012.

4   'a class of its own': Title of brochure issued by Kohinoor Group, undated.

4   'a mini metropolis': Advertisement for Sports City, *The Times of India*, Times Property, 23 February 2012.

4   'the answer to': Advertisement for Rising City, *Daily News and Analysis*, 25 October 2012.

4   'The eighth island': Advertisement for Island City Centre City, *Daily News and Analysis*, 15 September 2012.

6   'the meteoric growth': Ibid.

6   'ensure that the service staff': Advertisement for Island City Centre City, *The Times of India*, 15 September 2012.

6   'discover a better life': Ibid., 7 November 2012.

7   'a place where': *Two ICC*, brochure issued by The Wadia Group, undated.

7 'where business is discussed': Ibid.

TWO

14 'Many have been': Mrs Postans, *Western India in 1938, Vol I* (London: Saunders and Otley, 1839), p. 30.

14 'Bombay really': Govind Narayan, translated by Murali Ranganathan, *Govind Narayan's Mumbai: An Urban Biography from 1863* (UK and USA: Anthem Press, 2009), p. 134.

14 'Bombay is made': Ibid., p. 73.

16 'coastal microliths as': K. R. U. Todd, 'Palaeolithic Industries of Bombay', *The Journal of the Royal Anthropological Institute of Great Britain and Ireland, Vol 69*, No 2, 1939.

17 'Some of the': Ibid.

18 'Even Gautam Buddha': PTI, 'HC Stays Demolition of Tribal Woman's House near Stupa', *IBN Live*, 10 May 2012.

20 'one of the wonders': Partha Mitter, *Much Maligned Monsters: A History of European Reactions to Indian Art* (Chicago: The University of Chicago Press, 1992), p. 38.

20 'What is to': 'Glory and History Cave In: Can't Save Magathane', *The Indian Express*, 25 February 2010.

22 'a black stone': Stephen Meredyth Edwards, *The Rise of Bombay: A Retrospect* (Cambridge: Cambridge University Press, republished 2011), p. 35.

23 'the spirit of': Ibid.

24 'Different sorts of vows': K. Raghunathji, *The Hindu Temples of Bombay* (Bombay: Fort Printing Press, 1900), p. 230.

THREE

25 **'with all the fury'**: J. Gerson da Cunha, 'The Origin of Bombay', *The Journal of the Bombay Branch of the Royal Asiatic Society*, (Bombay: Royal Asiatic Society, 1900), p. 57.

25 **windowpanes in some homes**: Govind Narayan, translated by Murali Ranganathan, *Govind Narayan's Mumbai: An Urban Biography from 1863* (UK and USA: Anthem Press, 2009), p. 73.

26 **'milk was separated'**: Ibid., p. 85.

26 **'The building of'**: Ibid., p. 77.

27 **'My God!'**: Tony Palmer, *Charles II: Portrait of an Age* (London: Cassell, 1979), p. 61.

29 **'within a very'**: M. D. David, *History of Bombay* (Bombay: University of Bombay, 1973), p. 39.

29 **'in gold'**: John Stow and John Mottley, *A Survey of the Cities of London and Westminster, Borough of Southwark and Parts Adjacent* (London, printed for T Read, 1735), p. 434.

29 **'great burthen'**: John Keay, *The Honourable Company: A History of the English East India Company* (UK: HarperCollins, 1993), p. 134.

29 **'beggarly, ruined'**: Philip Anderson, *The English in Western India* (Bombay: Smith, Taylor and Co, 1854), p. 171.

29 **'poor little island'**: Samuel Pepys, *The Diary of Samuel Pepys, Vol VI* (New York: George E Croscup, 1893), p. 254.

29 **'inconsiderableness'**: Samuel Pepys, *Diary and Correspondence of Samuel Pepys, Vol IX-X* (UK: Dodd, 1887) p. 312.

29 **'no more than'**: John Ovington, *A Voyage to Suratt in*

the Year 1689 (London: Jacob Tonson, 1686), p. 142.

29 'two monsoons': Ibid.

30 'a city which': James Douglas, *Bombay and Western India: A Series of Stray Papers* (Bombay: Sampson Low, Marston & Co, 1893), p. 371.

30 'Our business is': John Keay, *The Honourable Company: A History of the English East India Company* (UK: HarperCollins, 1993), p. 136.

32 'recovering the overflown lands': James Campbell, *Materials Towards a Statistical Account of Town and Island of Bombay, Vol III* (Bombay: Government Central Press, 1894), p. 264.

32 'making soe much': Sir William Foster, *The English Factories in India, 1668-1669* (Oxford: Clarendon Press, 1927), p. 78.

32 'the coming in': Sir William Foster, *The English Factories in India, 1668-1669* (Oxford: Clarendon Press, 1927), p. 78.

33 'it will make good': Ibid.

33 'firm fast clay': John Burnell, *Bombay in the Days of Queen Anne* (London: Hakluyt Society, 1933), p. 70.

33 'covered with': Ibid.

34 'It is something': Ibid., p. 80.

34 'When I left': Ibid.

35 'grown scandalous': James Campbell, *Materials Towards a Statistical Account of Town and Island of Bombay, Vol I* (Bombay: Government Central Press, 1893), p. 79.

35 'in which confusedly': John Fryer, *A New Account of East India and Persia* (London: Hakluyt Society, 1909), p. 172.

35 'an industrious people': Stephen Meredyth Edwardes and James Campbell, *The Gazetteer of Bombay City and Island, Vol II* (Bombay: Times Press, 1909), p. 66.

36 'You are to suffer': Sir William Foster, *The English Factories in India, 1661-1664* (Oxford: Clarendon Press, 1927), p. 128.

36 'without fear': Mariam Dossal, *Theatre of Conflict, City of Hope* (New Delhi: Oxford University Press, 2010), p. xvii.

37 'The buckshawing': James Campbell, *Materials Towards a Statistical Account of Town and Island of Bombay, Vol III* (Bombay: Government Central Press, 1894), p. 501.

37 'The trees cannot': Ibid., p. 511.

38 'the health of': Ibid., p. 512.

39 'erected sheds': Ibid., p. 445.

40 'If anyone presume': Ibid.

40 'to raise their': Ibid., p. 492.

40 'a cure might': Ibid.

FOUR

41 'The streets are': Abraham Parsons, *Travels in Asia and Africa* (London: Longman, Hurst, Rees, and Orme, 1808), p. 216.

43 'Few places have': Mrs Postans, *Western India in 1938, Vol I* (London: Saunders and Otley, 1839), p. 2.

43 as the title: Madhavi Thampi and Shalini Saksena, *China and the Making of Bombay.* (Bombay: The K.R. Cama Oriental Institute, 2009).

46 'We had asked': Alisha Coelho, 'Several Squabbles Later, Sir JJ's Statue Will Finally Be Unveiled', *Mid-Day*, 15 July 2008.

47 'double walls': 'Cargo of Ice', *The Asiatic Journal and Monthly Register for British and Foreign India, China and Australasia*, January-April, 1835.

48 'the whole line': *Bombay Times*, 20 April 1853.

49 'Our pulses throbbed': D. E. Wacha, *Shells From the Sands of Bombay* (Bombay: K. T. Anklesaria, 1920), p. 80.

50 'to stimulate': Romesh Chunder Dutt, *The Economic History of India* (London: Routledge & Kegan Paul, 1969), p. 235.

50 'King Cotton was': D. E. Wacha, *A Financial Chapter in the History of Bombay City* (Bombay: AJ Combridge, 1910), p. 11.

50 'even old mattresses': Ibid.

51 'a large basket': Stephen Meredyth Edwardes and James Campbell, *The Gazetteer of Bombay City and Island, Vol II* (Bombay: Times Press, 1909), p. 154.

51 'devoted to regulating': Ibid., p. 170.

52 'from the highest': *Report of the Bombay Chamber of Commerce, 1861-62*, cited in Teresa Albuquerque, *Urbs Prima in Indis* (New Delhi: Promilla, 1985), p. 16.

52 'No enchanter': D. E. Wacha, *A Financial Chapter in the History of Bombay City* (Bombay: AJ Combridge, 1910), p. 47.

52 'The other shareholders': Gillian Tindall, *City of Gold* (New Delhi: Penguin Books, 1992), p. 176.

53 'with all the titanic': D. E. Wacha, *A Financial Chapter in the History of Bombay City* (Bombay: AJ Combridge, 1910), p. 211.

53 'It was a day': D. E. Wacha, *Premchund Roychund: His Early Life and Career* (Bombay: Times Press, 1913), p. 144.

53 'recalibrate [the] focus': 'It's the Prince of Wales' New Gallery and Everyone's Invited', *The Times of India*, 22 November 2002.

54 'The structure is': Govind Narayan, translated by Murali Ranganathan, *Govind Narayan's Mumbai: An Urban Biography from 1863* (UK and USA: Anthem Press, 2009), p. 206.

FIVE

56 'nothing is finer': *The Times of India*, 15 August 1878.

57 'Verily, the walls': James Douglas, *Bombay and Western India: A Series of Stray Papers* (Bombay: Sampson Low, Marston & Co, 1893), p. 225.

58 'threw out her': Ibid.

61 'The dead and': Edited by O. P. Brahmachary, *Economic Ideas of MG Ranade* (New Delhi: Deep and Deep Publications, 1995), p. 214.

62 'the riff-raff': Stephen Meredyth Edwardes, *The Bombay City Police* (Bombay: Oxford University Press, 1923), p. 85.

63 'ate the air': D. E. Wacha, *Shells From the Sands of Bombay* (Bombay: K. T. Anklesaria, 1920), p. 3.

63 'mat and lantern': K. N. Kabraji, 'Fifty Years Ago', *The Times of India*, 2 November 1901, p. 9.

63 'The members ate together': Ibid., p. 9.

63 'quite overrun with': D. Aubrey, *Letters from Bombay* (London: Remington and Co, 1884), p. 109.

64 'the resort...': Ibid., p. 74.

65 'to propagate among': Michael D. Rosse, 'Music Schools and Societies in Bombay c. 1864-1937' in *Hindustani Music: Thirteenth to Twentieth Centuries* (New Delhi: Manohar, 2010), p. 318.

SIX

69 'the hope of': K. Gopalaswami, *Gandhi and Bombay* (Bombay: Gandhi Smarak Nidhi, Bharatiya Vidya Bhavan, 1969), p. 125.

70 'a dozen families': Stephen Meredyth Edwards, *The Rise of Bombay: A Retrospect* (Cambridge: Cambridge University Press, republished 2011), p. 312.

71 'I don't like Bombay': K. Gopalaswami, *Gandhi and Bombay* (Bombay: Gandhi Smarak Nidhi, Bharatiya Vidya Bhavan, 1969), p. 26.

71 'Bombay is beautiful': Ibid., p. 151.

71 'It costs a lot': Hirendranath Mukherjee, *Gandhiji: A Study* (Bombay: People's Publishing House, 1979), p. 189.

73 'hooligans of Bombay': K. Gopalaswami, *Gandhi and Bombay* (Bombay: Gandhi Smarak Nidhi, Bharatiya Vidya Bhavan, 1969), p. 131.

75 'This mad and chimerical': Edited by K. K. Chaudhari, *Greater Bombay Gazetteer, Vol I* (Bombay: Gazetteers Department, 1986), p. 435.

77 'I am sure': *Mahatma Gandhi, The Collected Works of Mahatma Gandhi, Vol 76* (Delhi: Publications Division, 2000), p. 155.

78 **Parsi heiress Ruttie**: A company owned by Ruttie Jinnah's grandson is building Island City Centre. Jinnah's family home on Malabar Hill has been the subject of a bitter dispute between the Indian and Pakistani governments.

78 'Every attempt must': *Mahatma Gandhi, The Collected Works of Mahatma Gandhi, Vol 73* (Delhi: Publications Division, 2000), p. 190.

79 'Get out': Edited by K. K. Chaudhari, *Greater Bombay Gazetter, Vol I* (Bombay: Gazetteers Department, 1986), p. 543.

79 'Retreat': Ibid.

79 'Quit India': Ibid.

79 'Withdraw': Ibid.

79 'Amen': Ibid.

80 'Citizens of free': 'Frenzied Enthusiasm in Bombay', *The Times of India*, 15 August 1947.

80 'Hundreds of thousands': Ibid.

PART TWO

ONE

87 'anthropogenic structural': S. Gandhi, D. Mukherji, S. Srivastava, P. Gogate, *Study of Land Reclamation in Mumbai: Phase I (1970-2012)* (Mumbai: The Mumbai Transformation Unit Project, 2013), p. 4.

92 'Fourteen defenceless citizens': Quoted in Vaibhav Purandare, *The Sena Story* (Mumbai: Business Publications Inc, 1999), p. 375.

93 'Enough is enough': Ibid., p. 380.

TWO

102 'We have identified': Haima Deshpande, 'Shiv Sena's New Target: Vegetarian Housing Societies', *The Indian Express*, 16 April 2003.

THREE

103 'opulence personified': Company website, accessed at http://www.kohinoorsquare.in/inner.html

104 Four years later: Nauzer Bharucha, 'Raj Thackeray's Firm Made Rs 300 crore by Selling Stake in Mill', *Economic Times*, 15 November 2009.

105 'ready to bring': Quoted in Vaibhav Purandare, *The Sena Story* (Mumbai: Business Publications Inc, 1999), p. 39.

106 'rajkaran [politics] is': Ibid., p. 41.

109 'emasculation of the': Ibid., p. 85.

109 'sometimes thokshahi': Ibid., p 153.

112 'I have the *remote control*': 'Remote Control of Politics Remains With Me: Thackeray', *The Indian Express*, 23 January 2010.

FOUR

121 **'refusal to blink'**: Maharashtra Times Team, *50 Years Kohinoor* (Bombay: Bennett, Coleman And Company), p. 20.

FIVE

122 **'city of dreams'**: 'Obama Praises "City of Dreams" Mumbai', *Mid-Day*, 7 November 2010.

122 **'winding alleys'**: Ibid.

123 **'optimism and determination'**: Ibid.

124 **'the obvious'**: Rashmi Bansal and Deepak Gandhi, *Poor Little Rich Slum* (Chennai: Westland, 2012), p. 1.

124 **'We can be happy'**: Ibid.

128 **'capital accumulation'**: David Harvey, *The New Imperialism* (Oxford: Oxford University Press, 2003), p. 137.

129 **'opening out'**: Prashant Kidambi, *The Making of an Indian Metropolis*, (Aldershot: Ashgate Publishing Ltd, 2007), p. 71.

130 **'pseudo-sanitarians'**: 'Improvement Trust: A Vigorous Critic', *The Times of India*, 6 December 1912.

131 **'Bombay', said Geddes**: F. P. Antia, 'The City Dweller—A New Deal', *The Times of India*, 11 November 1962.

SIX

132 **'Mumbai on the Brink'**: *India Today*, 3 September 2012.

132 **'Who Killed'**: *Outlook*, 9 July 2012.

132 **'Urban CHAOS'**: *The Illustrated Weekly of India*, 1 September 1974.

133 **'Town planning'**: Patrick Geddes, *Patrick Geddes in India* (Bangalore: Select Books, 2007), p. 22.

136 'The effort has': Quoted in J. B. D'Souza, *No Trumpet or Bugles* (Mumbai: Allied Publishers, 2002), p. 183.
137 'the perfect complement': Company brochure, Shah Group.
137 'lavish work styles': Company brochure, Shelton Group.
138 'Bombay is a great': Charles Correa, *The New Landscape* (Bombay: The Book Society, 1985), p. 81.

SEVEN

142 most Bombay workers: Presentation at Guggenheim Urban Lab, Bhau Daji Lad Museum, Bombay, on 4 January 2013.

EIGHT

145 'been acquired at': Ammon Rodrigues, Letter to P. G. Kher, Mumbai, 9 February 1971.
147 'On these verdure-clad': Braz A. Fernandes, *Bandra: Its Religious and Secular History* (Bombay: D. K. Parker, 1927), p. 110.
148 'under the magic': Ibid., p. 4.
148 'cheap water supply': 'Town Planning Act: Mr Turner's Lecture', *The Times of India*, 12 August 1912.
148 'In this rush': Braz A. Fernandes, *Bandra: Its Religious and Secular History* (Bombay: D. K. Parker, 1927), p. 4.
150 'A man's home': Accessed at http://www.youtube.com/watch?v=HRDPzjzMiEM

NINE

154 'Yes, we need': 'Looking for Answers', *Time Out Mumbai*, 12-25 December 2008.

CPSIA information can be obtained
at www.ICGtesting.com
Printed in the USA
LVHW030824240122
709151LV00023B/1337/J